Catastrophe in Southern Asia:
The Tsunami of 2004

SWAMPSCOTT PUBLIC LIBRARY
Swampscott, Massachusetts 01907-1996

DISCARD

D0182099

Look for these and other books in the Lucent Overview series:

Abortion
Acid Rain
Adoption
AIDS
Bigotry
The Brain
Cancer
Chemical Dependency
Censorship
Cities
Civil Liberties
Cloning
Cults
The Death Penalty
Democracy
Divorce
DNA on Trial
Drug Abuse
Drugs and Sports
Drug Trafficking
Eating Disorders
Endangered Species
Epidemics
Environmental Groups
Espionage
Ethnic Violence
Euthanasia
Family Violence
Gambling
Gangs
Gay Rights
Global Resources
Gun Control

Hazardous Waste
Health Care
Homeless Children
Human Rights
Illegal Immigration
The Internet
Juvenile Crime
Legalizing Drugs
Mental Illness
Militias
Money
Multicultural America
Obesity
Oil Spills
The Palestinian-Israeli Accord
Paranormal Phenomena
Police Brutality
Population
Poverty
The Rebuilding of Bosnia
Saving the American Wilderness
Schools
Sexual Harassment
Sports in America
Suicide
Tattoos and Body Piercing
Terrorism
The U.S. Congress
The U.S. Presidency
Violence in the Media
Violence Against Women
Women's Rights
Zoos

Catastrophe in Southern Asia:
The Tsunami of 2004

by Gail B. Stewart

SWAMPSCOTT PUBLIC LIBRARY
Swampscott, Massachusetts 01907-1996

LUCENT BOOKS
An imprint of Thomson Gale, a part of The Thomson Corporation

THOMSON
™
GALE

Detroit • New York • San Francisco • San Diego • New Haven, Conn. • Waterville, Maine • London • Munich

© 2005 Thomson Gale, a part of The Thomson Corporation.

Thomson and Star Logo are trademarks and Gale and Lucent Books are registered trademarks used herein under license.

For more information, contact
Lucent Books
27500 Drake Rd.
Farmington Hills, MI 48331-3535
Or you can visit our Internet site at http://www.gale.com

ALL RIGHTS RESERVED.
No part of this work covered by the copyright hereon may be reproduced or used in any form or by any means—graphic, electronic, or mechanical, including photocopying, recording, taping, Web distribution, or information storage retrieval systems—without the written permission of the publisher.

Every effort has been made to trace the owners of copyrighted material.

LIBRARY OF CONGRESS CATALOGING-IN-PUBLICATION DATA

Stewart, Gail B., 1949–
  Catastrophe in Southern Asia : the Tsunami of 2004 / by Gail B. Stewart.
    p. cm. — (Overview series)
  Includes bibliographical references and index.
  ISBN 1-59018-831-4 (hard cover : alk. paper)
  1. Indian Ocean Tsunami, 2004—Juvenile literature. 2. Tsunamis—Indian Ocean—Juvenile literature. I. Title. II. Series: Lucent overview series.
  GC221.5.S76 2005
  909'.09824083—dc22

                                                          2005006036

Printed in the United States of America

Contents

Introduction
"My Heart Doesn't Have Enough Room"

TELEVISION HAS SHOWN the images from Indonesia, Sri Lanka, and Thailand. There have been shots of large wooden fishing boats in trees a quarter mile from the shore, trailer-trucks smashed like toys, and four-star hotels reduced to rubble. There have been shots of crying children whose parents were swept away, of weeping parents whose children were wrenched out of their arms and now are lost. Signs appear on every wall, every structure— "Have you seen my little girl? She has two teeth, and her name is Anja." "I am missing my son Hans. He speaks only Dutch and French. He has blue swimming trunks with Winnie the Pooh on them, and is very shy."

There have been shots of the dead, too—rows and rows of bright blue body bags laid out in public squares until family members can identify the remains. Such images are shocking, but those who lived through the earthquake and its aftermath—the giant waves, or tsunami, that tore through Southern Asia on December 26, 2004—say that television does not begin to convey the horror of the event.

The End of the World

One young woman from New Zealand tearfully told her parents that the coastal town in Sri Lanka where she was visiting reminded her of a painting she had once seen depicting the end of the world. Nothing was familiar, for there were no landmarks to indicate streets, markets,

Aerial photography shows the Indonesian city of Banda Aceh as it looked both before (above) and after (below) the devastating tsunami of December 26, 2004.

DigitalGlobe Photos

homes, or temples. Everywhere, she said, there was destruction and the smell of death.

A physician working in Banda Aceh, a city in Indonesia, says that "destruction" is too mild a word for what he saw. What was once a thriving city, he says, looks more like Hiroshima after the nuclear blast:

> It is as if someone took a rototiller to a city area seven miles wide and three miles deep, and ground it into bits and then flooded the uneven ground, creating ponds, inlets that drain to nowhere. . . . The United Nations has bulldozed some tracks across the rubble field that once was this city. The locals use them to try to find houses and mementos of their past lives. Relief helicopters . . . carrying supplies roar across the sky. The city smells of decomposition.[1]

Incalculable Loss

The disaster resulted in loss of every kind. As best as anyone can tell, 227,000 people died and at least 70,000 more are missing. Some of the dead and missing were tourists who had come from such faraway places as Sweden, the

Sri Lankans wade through the flooded rubble of their village. In addition to the large death toll, the tsunamis displaced over 5 million people in Southern Asia.

Netherlands, and England to enjoy vacations in Thailand. But the vast majority were citizens of Indonesia, Thailand, Sri Lanka, and India.

Experts explain that the exact death count may never be known, for entire villages were swept away, with no one remaining who might be able to tally the numbers accurately. In addition, there were believed to be at least one thousand construction workers from Myanmar killed in Thailand. Because they were working illegally without documentation, their identities may never be known.

In addition to the large numbers of dead, the quake and tsunami resulted in the displacement of more than five million people in Southern Asia. With stagnant water flooding towns, factories, and farmland, people had no choice but to relocate—in most cases to one of the makeshift refugee camps that opened soon after the disaster. And with overcrowded conditions and ineffective sewage systems in the camps, health workers feared outbreaks of disease that could wipe out as many people as the tsunami killed.

Infinite Sadness

Though the rest of the world pledged more than a billion dollars in aid for the stricken areas, many of the survivors quickly lost hope. The damage was so extensive—the loss of families and communities was too overwhelming. More than a month later, the searchers continued to retrieve dead bodies that had to be preserved until they could be identified.

In Sri Lanka, schools were being used as morgues, and two guards entrusted with keeping wild animals from the bodies said it was the most horrifying job they had ever done. The infinite sadness they felt when describing the bodies of young mothers still clutching their children, or babies with pacifiers still in their mouths, was evidence that nothing would be normal, ever again. They said that the expressions on the victims' faces will haunt them forever, no matter how much rebuilding is done in their city. "I'm very sad," says one. "It's just sadness from the day the waves hit until now. My heart doesn't have enough room to hold all this pain."[2]

1

"The Earth Shrugged for a Moment"

IRONICALLY, THE NATURAL disaster that resulted in so much death and destruction in Southern Asia was very unremarkable, at least in geological terms. After all, on a planet such as Earth, which has a molten core, entire continents have been destroyed by earthquakes, only to be reformed eons later. In planetary terms, notes geologist Simon Winchester, the event was "utterly insignificant. . . . The earth shrugged for a moment. Everything moved a little bit."[3]

Even so, the event was clearly a global one—not confined to a particular area. In fact, the earthquake that caused the tsunami was enough to affect the rotation of Earth so much that the day of December 26, 2004, was a few microseconds shorter than it should have been.

The Trigger

This particular earthquake occurred underwater, as most earthquakes do. Geologists who study earthquakes refer to the epicenter, or the point on Earth's surface directly above the quake's origin. The epicenter of this quake was in the Indian Ocean, just off the western coast of the island of Sumatra.

Large, rigid plates make up Earth's crust, ranging in depth from 4 miles to 40 miles (6.44 to 64.37km). These plates are in slow, continuous motion. This shifting motion produces friction between the plates and occasionally results in the edges of a plate breaking and shifting suddenly. The result is an unexpected movement, or quake, of the earth.

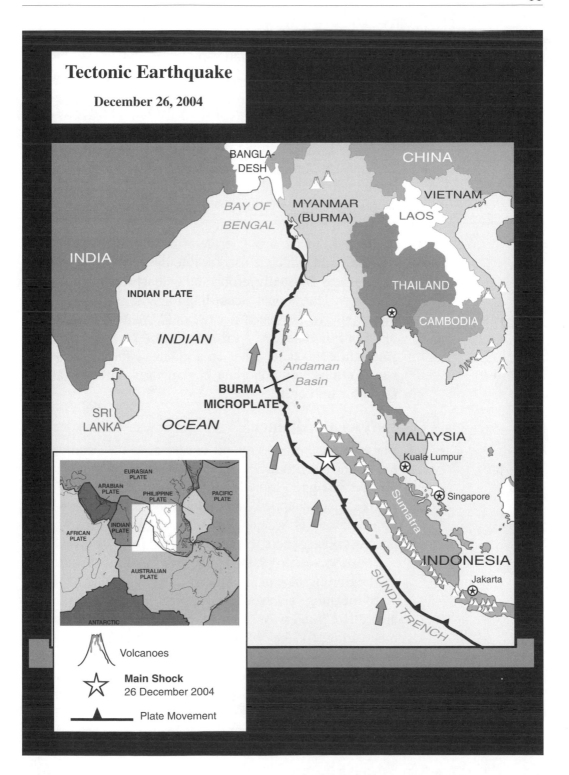

Tectonic Earthquake

December 26, 2004

CHINA
BANGLA-DESH
VIETNAM
BAY OF BENGAL
MYANMAR (BURMA)
LAOS
INDIA
INDIAN PLATE
THAILAND
CAMBODIA
INDIAN
Andaman Basin
BURMA MICROPLATE
SRI LANKA
OCEAN
MALAYSIA
Kuala Lumpur
Sumatra
Singapore
INDONESIA
Jakarta
SUNDA TRENCH

EURASIAN PLATE
ARABIAN PLATE
PHILIPPINE PLATE
PACIFIC PLATE
AFRICAN PLATE
INDIAN PLATE
AUSTRALIAN PLATE
ANTARCTIC

Volcanoes

Main Shock
26 December 2004

Plate Movement

The earthquake of December 2004 occurred because of grinding between two large plates in the Indian Ocean. One plate, known as the Indian plate, shifts north at the rate of about 2.5 inches (6.35cm) per year. As it moves, it is slowly forced underneath the Burma plate, to the east. The earthquake happened when the Burma plate suddenly snapped upward, toward the ocean surface, sliding about 50 feet (15.24m) at one time. The sudden friction caused more than 750 feet (228.6m) of the plate to break off. This violent motion 18 miles (29km) under the ocean was the cause of the massive earthquake.

The earthquake was later determined to be a 9.0 on the Richter scale, which is used to rate the force of a quake. A 9.0 quake is unusually strong and unleashes a huge amount of energy. The amount, according to geologists, is the same that would be produced if one could create a bomb made of 32 billion tons (29.03 metric tons) of TNT and set it off. And while the same event on a planet without human life would not be very important in planetary terms, it was catastrophic on Earth.

Fast as an Airliner

The earthquake was violent, but because it was underwater, it did not produce a great amount of damage. It did, however, trigger something far more deadly. When the Burma plate snapped, the sudden motion displaced trillions of tons of water. That mass of water drove to the ocean surface, where it spread outward in violent waves.

These waves, propelled by the energy of the quake, were the beginning of what is known as a tsunami, a Japanese word meaning "a wave in the harbor." Sometimes tsunamis are called "tidal waves," but experts say that this name is misleading, for they have nothing at all to do with tides. Tsunamis usually occur because of underwater earthquakes, although they can also be generated by coastal landslides, the impact of a meteor, or the eruption of an underwater volcano.

A tsunami beginning in deep ocean water travels in extremely long waves—sometimes the crests of the waves are

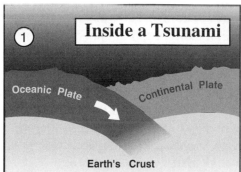

Inside a Tsunami

Most large tsunamis result from tectonic earthquakes. Extreme pressure builds when oceanic and continental plates press together. Eventually the heavier oceanic plate slips under the lighter continental plate and causes an underwater earthquake.

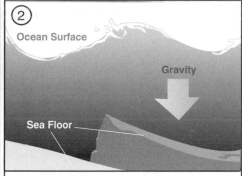

The earthquake lifts part of the ocean floor up and drops other parts down. What happens on the sea floor is mirrored on the ocean surface above; then gravity acts fast to quickly even out the water surface.

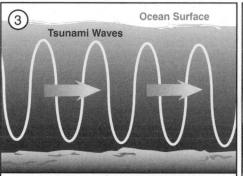

Even though the ocean surface looks flat, waves are moving through the ocean at speeds up to 600 miles per hour (956.61kmph). Tsunami waves carry a lot of energy and can extend thousands of feet deep. Tsunami waves also move a lot of water, so they can sometimes travel 10,000 miles (16,093km) or more.

When tsunami waves get close to shore they do not have the room they need to keep moving, so they slow down and pack together. Compacted waves cause the ocean to swell, forming a wall of water with a lot of energy inside.

Depending on the shape of the sea floor, the approaching tsunami will most often resemble a rapidly rising tide.

But some coastlines can slow the tsunami down enough to push it upward into a massive wave or series of waves, which is what happened in Southern Asia.

hundreds of miles apart. Astonishingly, these waves speed along under the surface of the ocean at speeds of near 600 miles per hour (956.61kmph), as fast as an airliner. Even though the water is moving at such a fast rate, however, it would be hardly noticeable to an airplane overhead or even a ship cruising above, for the waves on the surface appear insignificant— a few inches to 2 feet (60.9cm) in height.

Reaching Shallow Water

It is when the tsunami reaches shallower water near land that it becomes visibly threatening. The waves slow, the length of the waves shortens, and their height increases, sometimes to 100 feet (30.48m) or more. The force of the wave is so strong that it can flood areas 1,000 feet (304.8m) from the shoreline. This shifting of shape and intensity from silent underwater speed to massive wall of water is what makes tsunamis so dangerous.

A tsunami "can be literally a bolt from the blue," says geologist Paul Meyer. "It seems to come out of nowhere. The sky can be clear, the sun shining. No storms, not like getting hit with a hurricane or a bolt of lightning. People can be sitting on the seashore, getting some sun, relaxing with the kids, fishing, whatever. And suddenly, there's a 45-foot wave pounding onto the beach. They didn't have a chance."[4]

Even seasoned sailors are appalled by the suddenness of tsunamis. When a tsunami hit Hawaii in 1946, crew members of ships that were lying a mile or two off the coast could see the gigantic breaking waves slamming into the shore, but they could detect nothing where they were— only the gentle rise and fall of the sea's surface.

Sumatra First

The tsunami of December 2004 first hit the northern end of the Indonesian island of Sumatra. Because that region was close to the epicenter of the quake, it suffered damage from both the earthquake and the tsunami. Bustami, a fisherman from Sumatra, was in his boat when the quake hit. He felt the sea moving strangely around him at about 8:00

A.M. "That must have been when the earthquake hit," he says. About thirty minutes later, he felt the shock wave of the tsunami. "I heard this strange thunderous sound from somewhere," he recalls, "a sound I'd never heard before. I thought it was the sound of bombs."[5]

Bustami was thrown out of his boat when the water rose behind him—higher even than the coconut trees along the shore. He snagged hold of one of the trees and hung on until he was rescued three hours later. He was lucky, for tens of thousands of people in villages near his were killed by the waves. In Indonesia as a whole, 166,000 people are believed to have died.

After battering Sumatra, the tsunami sped to the Thailand coast, about 300 miles (482.8km) from the earthquake's epicenter, and then to India and Sri Lanka a few hours later. Within seven hours, the tsunami had reached the east coast of Africa—3,000 miles (4,828km) away. In its wake it left behind hundreds of thousands dead, at least as many missing, and a landscape that was scarred and unrecognizable. Whole coastlines changed within a few minutes, and islands disappeared.

Tidal waves crash through houses on a beach in southern Sri Lanka. The waves killed thousands of people in Sri Lanka.

No Warning?

Geology experts quickly surmised that the catastrophe of December 26, 2004, was one of the most deadly natural events in modern history. That said, however, a disturbing question arose immediately after the disaster, voiced by people not only in Southern Asia, but throughout the world: With all of the geological and seismological (relating to earthquakes) warning systems in existence, why was the loss of life so heavy? Why were people not warned before it was too late?

The most significant reason is that among the nations that ring the Indian Ocean there is an utter lack of technology that could have picked up signs of a tsunami in an accurate, timely manner. Tsunami technology exists, but in the Pacific Ocean, rather than in the Indian Ocean. Experts say that is because more than 90 percent of tsunamis occur

This buoy located in the Pacific Ocean is part of a tsunami early warning system. Unfortunately, few countries in Southern Asia can afford such a warning system.

in the Pacific. "So nations that sit on the Pacific Ocean got together to form the Pacific Tsunami Warning Center in 1965," says one geologist. "Besides that, you've got countries who've had destructive tsunamis that have their own warning systems. Australia's got one; so does Japan. And since the United States has experienced tsunamis in the Pacific—one in Hawaii and one that affected Alaska, Oregon, and California in 1964—we've got our own system in place, too."[6]

Even though a tsunami is an exceedingly rare event in the Indian Ocean, however, scientists in other parts of the world actually did have some information about the earthquake and tsunami before either had claimed any lives. And a few of those scientists attempted to issue warnings, but most went either unnoticed or unheeded. A combination of things prevented a warning from getting to the people most vulnerable to the disaster—a lack of a communications network, a rigid international bureaucracy, and simple errors in judgment.

Priorities

Tsunami warning systems cost a great deal of money, and for many nations bordering the Indian Ocean, a warning system for such a rare occurrence had never seemed like an important investment. With the social and financial problems many of these nations face, spending millions of dollars on equipment to detect tsunamis seemed like a low priority.

Besides, even the most experienced geophysicists acknowledge that even with high-tech equipment, predicting tsunamis is hardly easy. As tsunami expert Dr. Laura Kong says, "It's an inexact science now."[7] Every earthquake does not automatically trigger a tsunami, she says, and even when water is displaced and tsunami waves form, the waves can end up only inches high—hardly a threat to a coastal community.

In fact, since 1948, about 75 percent of tsunami warnings in the Pacific have been unnecessary—the waves did arrive and were often a bit higher than normal, but caused

Initially, experts at Hawaii's Pacific Tsunami Warning Center believed that the undersea earthquake in the Indian Ocean would not generate a tsunami.

little or no damage to the shore. Experts say that a tsunami may appear to be dangerous, but the configuration of the ocean floor or the shape of a bay may weaken its impact by the time it reaches land. When that many warnings turn out to be false, say experts, people stop responding to them.

False warnings are very costly, too, especially for places that rely heavily on tourism. Evacuating a popular vacation spot like Hawaii, for example, would result in the loss of about $68 million per day in tourism and workers' productivity.

"We Wanted to Try to Do Something"

Interestingly, the quake was powerful enough that sensors in Japan and Australia—both close to the Indian Ocean—detected the tremors first, just minutes after the quake. Because it occurred outside the Pacific area, information about the underwater quake from monitors was sketchy. However, the event was significant enough so the Pacific Tsunami Warning Center (PTWC) in Hawaii was alerted, and geophysicist Stuart Weinstein dispatched a bulletin to countries around the Pacific Rim, including Thailand and Indonesia. The message was: "This earthquake is located outside the Pacific. No destructive tsunami threat exists based on historical earthquake and tsunami data."[8]

By the time experts in the Pacific realized that the earthquake was a "monster quake" far more intense than first thought and that a tsunami was indeed likely, it was too late for the people in North Sumatra. Thousands of people in a remote part of the island were killed instantly. It was not until the tsunami had spread to Sri Lanka, south of India, and was reported in breaking news bulletins that the experts in the Pacific realized what had occurred.

But by that time, they say, there was little they could do, other than to continue to monitor the path of the killer wave. They had no system in place that provided an emergency list of the right people to call. "We wanted to try to do something," says PTWC head Dr. Charles McCreery, "but without a plan in place then, [there] was not an effective way to issue a warning, or to have it acted upon."[9]

A lone mosque stands among the tsunami damage of a village on Sumatra.

Certainly there was no guarantee that if officials in Southern Asia had received such a warning it would have done much good. Scientists in Thailand, for example, had received updates about the strength of the earthquake during the morning, but did not act upon that information. One scientist in Bangkok says that there was no sense of urgency, simply because the quake was far away from Thailand. "In the past one thousand years we've never had a tsunami," he says, "so why should I issue a warning for one?"[10]

"Yes, We Messed Up"

Even so, many scientists that had tracked the disaster on December 26 feel frustration. They admit that because they had information they were not able to communicate, they feel a huge sense of responsibility for the loss of life. "Did we mess up?" asks one earthquake specialist irritably. "Yes, we messed up. One hundred and sixteen thousand human beings [this total was later revised] are dead."[11]

Just a few hours after the disaster, United Nations officials solemnly promised that its top priority for 2005 would be to link all the nations in Southern Asia with the Pacific Ocean network for tsunami warnings. However, for hundreds of thousands of people on that morning of December 26, 2004, it was too late.

2

"I Shall Never Forget the Screaming"

FOR MANY WHO lived through the tsunami, the first clue that there was anything wrong was the water itself—even before a wave appeared. The color changed drastically. Water off the Thai coast, which usually appeared a brilliant turquoise, suddenly turned white and frothy. In Sri Lanka, say observers, the water went from a sparkling green "to a dark, menacing black, as if it were filled with oil."[12]

"I've Never Seen Anything Like It in the Movies"

Very soon after noticing a change in color, people noticed a change in the movement of the water, too. Instead of steady tide lapping at the shore, the water seemed to be churning and moving in the wrong direction.

In Banda Aceh, a town in northern Sumatra that was close to the quake's epicenter, the deputy mayor knew something was odd when he went to the market. As he glanced out to sea, he noticed something very odd that he had never seen before. The water line appeared to be dipping down on the sides and rising rapidly in the middle. "The water separated," he says, "and then it attacked. I've never seen anything like it in the movies. I couldn't imagine anything like it."[13]

Off the coast of India, a fisherman noticed the same thing. The change happened very fast. "That morning, the sea was like it always was," he says. "Then suddenly it was

Satellite photos show the initial retreating wave moving away from a Sri Lankan beach (above).
Minutes later the deadly wave slams into the shoreline (below).

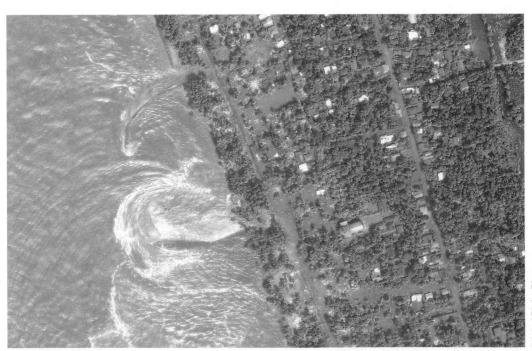

DigitalGlobe Photos

on fire. Boiling. It lifted up eleven yards and paused, almost like it was surveying us below it. And then it fell. It consumed one house after another, like paper boxes."[14]

Beaches with No Water

One phenomenon that was widely reported was a strange wave that actually went in reverse, moving quickly away from shore, rather than toward it. Geologists refer to that as a retreating wave, explaining that if the trough, or bottom, of a tsunami arrives on land first, before the crest, it actually retreats, sucking water out to sea.

In Sri Lanka, a hotel manager recalls the odd picture of a beach with no water and hundreds of gorgeous, colorful fish stranded on the sandy bottom. The first impulse of the fishermen was to grab the fish before the water returned and they swam away. "Men ran down to the shore with gunny-bags," he says, "and stuffed them full of fish."[15]

In northern Sumatra, a large wave receded a full forty yards immediately after the quake. Onlookers say that children and even some adults ran out into the seabed to collect the fish that flopped helplessly there. However, when the crest of the wave came, at least one hundred people were swept away instantly. One fisherman is haunted by the image. "I shall never forget the screaming of those being washed out to sea."[16]

Running from the Wave

When the wave's crest approached the shore and reared up to its full height, people who had moments before been transfixed by the retreating wave ran in panic. But the tsunami was faster than any of them could run. Tens of thousands at a time were slammed by the wall of water and killed instantly. In one coastal town of India, bodies of fish sellers from a local market were found 2 miles (3.22km) inland from where they had been working. Others were knocked off their feet and, unable to rise, drowned in the brackish water. In Sri Lanka, a man watched as dozens of buses filled with passengers were submerged by the tsunami, killing everyone inside.

Malayan villagers walk among hundreds of deep-ocean fish washed ashore by the tsunami.

Some survived by the sheer fortune of grabbing hold of something high or strong. One woman climbed into the top branches of a tree and stayed there for six hours. A little boy held onto a car bumper as he watched his mother, father, and sisters being swept away. Sutrisono, a fisherman from Sumatra, managed to get his wife and child to the roof of their home, watching with horror as most of the homes in their village were destroyed.

One Banda Aceh man who spent most of his time near the water survived simply because he was curious. He had heard that the earthquake shortly before had destroyed an entire block of stores downtown, and he went inland—away from the water—to see. "I was looking at the building," he says, "and I turned around to see the water coming into the city from two directions. The waves looked empty, but on top they were carrying everything from cars to the roofs of houses. I ran."[17]

Running Toward the Waves

Ironically, some of the survivors were people who did not run from the waves. Casey Sobolewski and his mother, Julie, vacationing in Thailand from Oceanside, California, had chartered a 35-foot (10.67m) boat that morning. It was hot and sunny—a great day for a sail, they thought.

They were about a mile from shore, heading to a sandbar on a little island where about one hundred people were sunbathing and enjoying the beautiful weather. Suddenly, says Julie, a wall of water 30 feet (9.14m) high appeared out of

This scene of flooded devastation is nearly 2 miles (3.22km) from the beach. Throughout Southern Asia, the tsunamis leveled villages miles from shore.

nowhere and inundated the sandbar. "It looked like the top half of the island was falling into the ocean," she says. She and Casey watched as the wave swallowed up the people. "They disappeared," she says.

As the water turned choppy and wild, Julie and Casey were appalled to see a wave demolish a group of long wooden boats nearby. "When [the wave] hit the five boats, they just exploded," she says, "and all of a sudden there were 35 people floating in the water."[18]

They realized they could not outrun the wave, Julie says, and so they decided to sail directly into it. The wave had been slowed somewhat by the sandbar, and the loss of its power allowed them to slice through the water. They spent the next six hours pulling from the sea survivors who had been sucked toward their boat by the retreating wave.

"Like a Nuclear Bomb Hit"

Two other vacationers were scuba diving nearby, 120 feet (36.38m) underwater, when the tsunami hit. They had no idea what was happening at the time, only that there was suddenly a very heavy current and that they could no longer see anything underwater.

When they got into their boat to head back to shore, they were puzzled by what looked like garbage strewn on the water. "We still didn't know what had happened," one diver says. "Then we started seeing things in the water. It looked like trash. But I saw furniture, TV sets and refrigerators floating by. Then we started seeing bodies."[19]

As they approached what had been a dock, they saw the aftermath of the tsunami—dead bodies, with clothing ripped off by the waves. On the beach, cats and dogs and children's toys were everywhere, and people were screaming. One palm tree had a speedboat impaled on it upside down; another had a dead baby in its branches. The scene looked, the divers said, "like a nuclear bomb hit. There are parts where nothing is left, there are feet and feet of rubble. And bodies are everywhere."[20]

Their horror was echoed by a television reporter in India who was witnessing similar scenes. "Seen things I never

Many of those killed by the tsunami were children. This Indonesian girl and her baby brother were among the children who survived.

thought I'd see," he e-mailed. "Seen things I don't ever want to see again. How do you ask a question of a father who saw his four-year-old child being dragged off into the sea and be sensitive about it?"[21]

Trying to Save the Children

Some of the most heartbreaking accounts concerned parents trying desperately to save their children. A woman in Sri Lanka ran into a local temple with her four young grandchildren, hoping they would be spared. She secured them by tying them to a heavy beam in the back of the temple and ran back out to bring other children to what she believed was a refuge from the waves. Onlookers watched helplessly as the wave that swept her away rushed into the temple, too, and drowned the children inside.

In Kahawa, on the south coast of Sri Lanka, a train filled with travelers stopped when the first wave hit. "Perhaps," says one observer, "its engineer thought stopping was safer than moving on."[22] When the first wave subsided, retreating back to the sea, many local people ran out to the train and put their children aboard, hoping they would be safe in the heavy cars. However, two more waves hit, each higher than the last, and the cars were picked up and knocked into trees and buildings. Almost none of the more than fifteen hundred passengers on board survived—including the children of Kahawa.

"No Idea in This Big World"

One visitor to Thailand from New York City was struck by the oddness of the scenes he witnessed. He recalled bits of detail that did not seem to go together, especially the different reactions of wealthy tourists and native people, yet it all was part of the same disaster. "Kids missing and sharks washed ashore, and people worrying about the Christian Dior shirts and jewels while people were being thrown against rocks," he says. "It was just so random."[23]

Randomness could also describe who lived and who died in the disaster. It did not always matter whether one was strong or weak, young or old. An entire group of able-bodied boys playing cricket on an Indian beach were swept away by a single wave, and a seventy-two-year-old grandmother in Sri Lanka was found alive high atop a palm tree. Her leg was broken, and she had no recollection of how she got there. Teens who were excellent swimmers drowned in the waves, and an entire church filled with Sunday morning worshippers was swept away.

Inexplicably, however, a twenty-day-old baby was found alive, floating alone on a mattress. Although the child was sunburned and hungry, rescuers pronounced her healthy.

"You ask me how such a thing is possible," a fisherman who spotted the infant says, weeping, "and I say, I have no idea. No idea in this big world."[24]

Ancient Instincts

Equally perplexing is the high survival rate among certain groups of people in the afflicted regions. On India's Andaman and Nicobar islands, for example, are five indigenous tribes who live much as their ancient ancestors did. They rub stones together to get fire and use bows and arrows to fish and hunt. They have almost no contact with the outside world.

Normally, they would be living in huts near the sea in late December, for the fishing is extremely good then. However, hours before the waves hit, they knew to move inland and to higher ground. "They can smell the wind," says one local environmentalist. "They can gauge the depth of the sea with the sound of their oars. They have a sixth sense which we don't possess."[25]

For centuries the Moken tribe has lived on an island off Thailand. Observing the unusually low tide before the first tsunami, the Moken moved inland to safety.

Another aboriginal people, the Mokens, live on South Surin Island, 40 miles (64.37km) off the coast of Thailand, and they, too, had foreknowledge of the tsunami. Sometimes called Sea Gypsies, the Moken have lived as fishermen, isolated from other cultures, for many generations. Their chief, Mr. Salama, explains that legends about the "people-eating wave" have been passed down orally from their ancestors by tribal elders. When he saw the unusually low tide before the first tsunami wave, he knew this was trouble. He ran through the village, shouting to people to run inland. Only one elderly man was caught by the waves; the rest of the Mokens survived.

Animals Knew

Scientists noted, too, that the animal populations of the regions survived extraordinarily well. "No elephants are dead, not even a dead hare or rabbit," said a Sri Lankan wildlife expert. "I think animals can sense disaster. They know when things are happening."[26]

In Indonesia eight elephants that were part of a tourist ride were credited with saving the lives of a dozen visitors the morning of the tsunami. Immediately after the earthquake, say observers, the elephants began shifting nervously and trumpeting—something they do only when frightened. Even though their trainer calmed them, they bolted for higher ground—just moments before the first tsunami wave hit—with their frightened passengers clinging to the baskets on the elephants' backs. Had they stayed on the regular track, the animals and their riders would have certainly been killed.

Some indigenous animals, like these rabbits, were aware of the approaching tsunami danger.

"I Didn't Want to Let Go"

Relatively few people, however, were lucky enough to have an early warning. For the vast majority of people, the tsunami was a monstrously destructive force that was completely unexpected. No one knew for certain when the danger had passed.

"All we could think about at the time was whether another [tsunami wave] was coming," says one woman from a coastal town in India. "I wanted to look for my husband and my brother, but I didn't want to let go of the tree I was holding. I thought I could be swept away if another wave came."[27]

A woman from Meulaboh, the town on Sumatra closest to the epicenter of the quake, knows firsthand that the tsunami was not confined to one wave. When the tsunami hit, she and her family scrambled up a tree to escape. However, after two more waves, each more powerful than the last, they moved to the roof of their house. Three more waves washed the family away in different directions. The sixth wave carried her to the local mosque, where she clung for hours to the steeple, or minaret, until she felt it was safe to look for her husband and children.

She says that she was lucky that her children were all found. Her younger son, the last to be found, had spent two days clinging to a mattress and ended up being rescued by a soldier. "He was so excited," she says. "He thought I was dead."[28]

"Everyone Is Asking the Same Questions"

Finding family members and friends was the first priority once the tsunami ended. It was especially difficult because in afflicted regions, the entire landscape had changed. In Meulaboh, for example, most of the town was underwater. "It is completely drowned," says one survivor. "Meulaboh has become like an ocean."[29]

Many homes and shops were gone altogether; those that remained were missing entire walls or roofs. Roads lay far under the brackish water. It was hard for survivors looking for loved ones to even know where to start. "I am looking

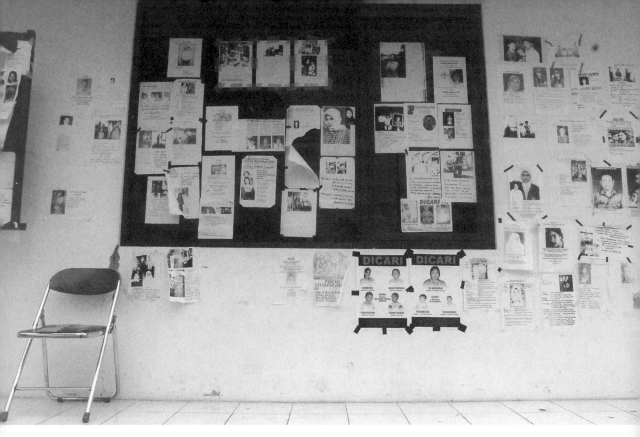

Flyers asking for information on missing persons crowd the wall of a hospital in Bandah Aceh, Indonesia. Thousands of people were never found.

for my three sisters," one teenager told a reporter sadly. "I already know my mother and father are dead. But I'm hoping they are alive somewhere."[30]

One Australian woman says that it was difficult to watch the faces of the people who were searching, especially those seeking their lost children:

> You'd see someone wild with worry, someone who lost track of their son or daughter. And they'd go up to everyone saying, "Did you see my child?" or whoever it was. It was so painful.

> It seemed like each person was asking the same questions as everyone else, over and over. "Did you see him? He had on a blue baseball hat, and he was holding my hand, and suddenly he was gone." It was over and over. You felt so bad, you wanted to be able to say, "Yes, your little boy is over there, he's fine." But you had no idea, you know? I told my husband, I'd give anything to give someone good news. But there just wasn't much of that, was there?[31]

Treating the Wounded

Makeshift hospitals were set up in structures that were still standing. Large numbers of people were brought in, suffer-

ing from deep cuts and lacerations from flying debris—
tree branches, broken glass, shards of metal. Others struggled to breathe, their lungs filled with salt water.

Those who were not injured helped by building temporary bridges over sink holes, and volunteers formed crews
to carry the wounded to shelters. Without stretchers, they
used doors or rigid box spring mattresses to transport the
victims.

The hospitals were barely staffed—especially in Indonesia, where so many health care workers had died in the
tsunami. Anyone with a background in science or nursing
was pressed into service, setting broken legs, bandaging

Aid stations and makeshift shelters like this one in Indonesia provided some relief to tsunami survivors, but their resources were quickly exhausted.

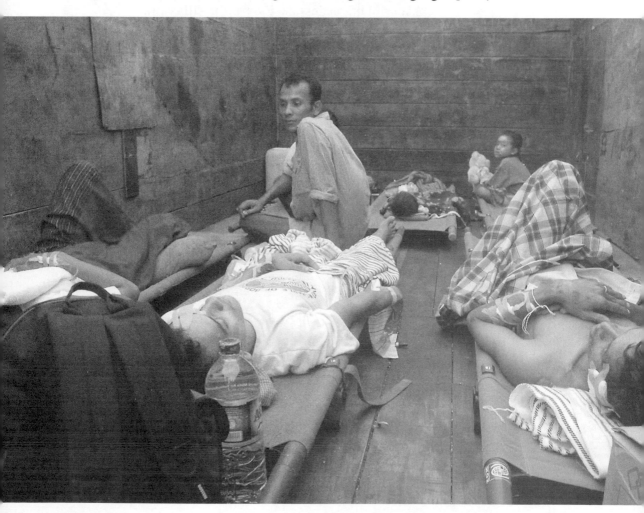

cuts, and so on. They lacked antibiotics and painkillers, however, and they cut up sheets from hotel beds to use as bandages. Workers with medical backgrounds said that the care they were giving, while it was the best they could do, was very limited.

As difficult as it was helping the injured, it was becoming increasingly clear that another huge problem lay ahead. In the days directly after the disaster, there were more than 100,000 bodies of tsunami victims strewn across Southern Asia, and there would be at least that many more recovered in weeks and months to come. Dealing with the sheer numbers of corpses—retrieval, identification, and disposal—was a grim but necessary job for the survivors.

3

Dealing with
the Dead

SOON AFTER THE WAVES subsided, there were hundreds, thousands, tens of thousands of bodies throughout the affected areas in Southern Asia. Some lay on the shore; others had been tossed by the waves under cars or trucks or into the branches of trees. Most were naked, or nearly so—the water had literally torn the clothing from their bodies. Some of the bodies were horribly mutilated from colliding with rocks or trees, while others, said one observer, "look quietly asleep."[32]

Mass Graves and Crematoria

In most of the affected regions of Southern Asia, the bodies of the tsunami's victims were alarmingly abundant. The presence of so many bodies created a health hazard. To avoid the spread of disease, rescue workers across Southern Asia began disposing of the bodies hundreds—or even thousands —at a time.

In India and Sri Lanka, for example, local relief workers hauled corpses out of villages that had been flattened by the waves and stacked them like firewood on large wagons. They were taken to hastily built crematoria—large fires accelerated by diesel fuel that burned the bodies to ash.

Indonesia, on the other hand, is a Muslim nation, and Islam forbids cremation of the dead. Muslim teaching states that bodies must be buried, but only after they are carefully washed and then wrapped in white cloth. After the tsunami, however, religious authorities issued a special fatwa, or

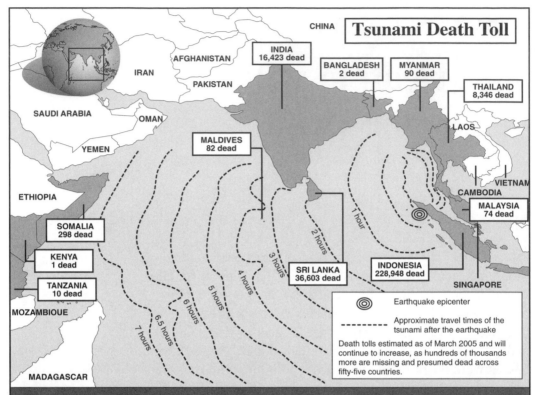

Tsunami Death Toll

CHINA

INDIA
16,423 dead

AFGHANISTAN

BANGLADESH
2 dead

MYANMAR
90 dead

IRAN

PAKISTAN

THAILAND
8,346 dead

SAUDI ARABIA

OMAN

LAOS

YEMEN

MALDIVES
82 dead

VIETNAM

CAMBODIA

ETHIOPIA

MALAYSIA
74 dead

SOMALIA
298 dead

1 hour

2 hours

3 hours

SRI LANKA
36,603 dead

INDONESIA
228,948 dead

SINGAPORE

KENYA
1 dead

4 hours

5 hours

TANZANIA
10 dead

MOZAMBIQUE

6 hours

6.5 hours

7 hours

MADAGASCAR

◎ Earthquake epicenter

------- Approximate travel times of the tsunami after the earthquake

Death tolls estimated as of March 2005 and will continue to increase, as hundreds of thousands more are missing and presumed dead across fifty-five countries.

On December 26, 2004, the Burma plate (a very small tectonic plate located between the Eurasian and Indian plates) suddenly jolted about 60 feet (18.28m), causing a 9.0 magnitude earthquake centered off the coast of northern Indonesia. The plate movement also caused the seafloor to be uplifted and shifted by several feet, generating a series of large waves called tsunami. The tsunami traveled thousands of miles across the Indian Ocean, generating waves on the coasts up to 50 feet (15.24m) high, killing hundreds of thousands of people and causing massive destruction.

edict. Because of the large number of dead in Indonesia, and because of the perceived health threat posed by so many decaying bodies, the rules could be relaxed somewhat. The bodies did not need to be wrapped in cloth, and instead of washing individual bodies, a holy man sprinkled water on them before bulldozers covered the large graves with dirt. Some mass graves in Indonesia contained more than thirty-seven hundred bodies.

A More Serious Danger

A few days after mass burnings and burials had started, health authorities at the Word Health Organization (WHO) advised rescue workers to stop the disposal of the bodies. Unless the bodies were lying in a water supply, WHO officials said, there was no danger of their spreading disease. In fact, by disposing of the bodies so quickly, rescue workers were unintentionally creating a situation that might be far more dangerous to the survivors—in a psychological sense.

Experts at WHO felt that to come to grips with the profound loss so many had suffered, it was crucial to allow family members to identify the remains of loved ones, if possible. According to one WHO communication, instead of burying or burning the corpses, rescue workers should make every effort to find all the victims and to give families "the opportunity to conduct funerals and burials according to social custom."[33] So the fires and mass burials were halted, and the grueling process of collection and identification continued.

Wearing masks to filter out the stench from decomposing bodies, volunteers help remove the dead from the streets of their village.

Finding the Dead

Although most of the bodies were found close to the seashore, so they were quite easy to recover, others had been carried far inland by the waves, and it was often difficult to locate them. There were many reports of people returning to their homes and finding the bodies of strangers lying inside.

One Indonesian man returned to his ruined house days after the tsunami and was horrified to find the body of a small boy, arms extended, with eyes open. "He's the same age as my son," sobbed the man. "He's lost too. Why do they have to leave him here to remind me?"[34]

Some of the bodies had been flung to more remote locations. And because most roads had been washed away, getting to such areas was impossible. Many workers worried that by the time they were able to travel inland to search for victims, many of the bodies would have been eaten or carried away by wild animals.

"We Need Elephant Power"

In Thailand, the tsunami was so strong that some victims were carried more than a mile (1.61km) from shore, deep into the jungle. While special dogs were brought into those remote areas to locate bodies, they were largely ineffective, perhaps due to the difficult terrain. However, one rescue worker found that elephants had far more success in the jungle.

"We need elephant power," she explained, "because there are things we can't move, places where heavy equipment can't go. With the elephant, we get two for one. They can also help move bodies. . . . Before we got an elephant, we moved a body two kilometers through the jungle [about 1.25 miles]. My staff could not walk after that in the tropical heat."[35]

A trainer stayed with the elephant as it moved through the heavy vegetation, and when the elephant located a victim, the trainer wrapped the body in a plastic body bag. On a command from the trainer, the elephant gently picked up

the bag and carried it down an overgrown jungle path to a waiting wagon. One reporter was amazed as he watched an elephant named Plai Sudor navigate the most difficult terrain to transport a body to where the workers were waiting: "Up to his knees in mud, Plai Sudor gently pushed aside a car to reveal a tsunami victim lost in a lagoon. Lumbering down a jungle path, [he] carried, slung from his tusks, a green plastic bag loaded with a 200-pound body."[36]

Trained elephants in Thailand helped locate and transport bodies during cleanup operations after the tsunami.

"Smashed Like a Potato Chip"

While the retrieval of bodies was difficult in the jungles of Thailand, it was virtually impossible in one Indonesian village called Calang, on the southwest coast of Sumatra near the quake's epicenter. A village of about seventy-three hundred people, Calang is bordered by the Indian Ocean on two sides, and although most of its citizens are believed to have perished in the tsunami, there are almost no traces of them. Rescue workers found a few bodies near the shore immediately after the tsunami, but most of the people have disappeared, most likely swept out to sea.

In neighboring villages, corpses lay on the ground by the hundreds, but one man said he was not surprised that Calang's inhabitants had disappeared. He had been standing on the top of a hill above his own village when the tsunami came, and he saw three large waves hit Calang. The force of the tsunami, hitting from two sides at once, was not likely to result in survivors. "When the waves came," he says, "the coconut trees just smashed like a potato chip in your hand."[37]

Dignity and Apologies

Sri Lankans pick their way through the rubble of their town's main street. More than a month after the tsunami, thousands of bodies were still being found every day.

In most of the affected regions, however, bodies were much in evidence. More than a month after the tsunami, workers in some areas of Indonesia were still finding more than one thousand bodies a day. As that number began to drop, though, it was not a sign that most of the victims had been picked up—only that they were becoming harder

to find. "It's difficult to find them now," says one Red Cross worker, "because a lot of them are under houses, under the rubble."[38]

The job was difficult, both physically and psychologically. The tropical heat speeded up the putrification process, a natural occurrence in which the flesh of the body decays. "In the first week, the smell was not so bad," says one disaster relief worker. "With a simple mask and simple gloves, they could handle it."[39] But after two or three weeks, he says, it became far more difficult. The smell had intensified so that workers required industrial-grade masks to filter out the stench, and the bodies tended to come apart.

Police, soldiers, Red Cross personnel, and other workers (including many volunteers) came up with ways of coping with the terrible reality of so many dead. One volunteer found it helpful to preserve the dignity of the victim by speaking to the body he was retrieving: "He has only lost his body," says the worker, a man named Mr. Ramza. "His soul is still there. I was talking to his soul." Ramza, like many other volunteers, says he decided to help with the retrieval of bodies for a very specific reason. "I am doing this for my parents," he explains, "because I can't find them."[40]

"Her Face Was Changed"

Identifying the bodies of loved ones was a grueling process. Just as people created makeshift hospitals in the hours after the tsunami, authorities set up makeshift morgues. Bodies were brought to a central location in each village or town—usually a temple or school that had not received much damage.

The bodies were laid out in rows, sometimes hundreds at a time. Workers tried to separate bodies of tourists from the rest, so that there was some sort of order. Some sites had coffins, but when they ran out of those, workers used body bags or plastic sheeting to cover the bodies. Even though dry ice was heaped on top of the plastic to slow down decomposition, damage to the body from water and heat made it very difficult for survivors to identify a family member.

One young man from Sri Lanka searched for four days before finding the body of his mother. He said it was almost impossible to recognize her. "Her body went out to sea and came back," he explains sadly, "and her face was changed."[41]

Workers at the morgues say that families had mixed feelings as they arrived. Some had been making the rounds of hospitals, hoping desperately to find that their loved one had survived and was merely injured. After weeks of doing that, they made the decision to try the morgue. One worker says that people showed very different emotions when faced with identifying a body.

"People would have hopes in their eyes until the tarps were unwrapped [by a morgue worker] and the faces were shown, and then they would cover their mouths and cry," he says. "Most were hoping the bodies weren't the ones they were looking for, while some were just hoping to find closure on their missing friends and relatives."[42]

Forensic Teams

Technicians and morgue workers tried to make the process of identification a little easier by taking a photograph of each victim and stapling it to the coffin or body bag. The bodies were coming in faster than they could be identified, however, and it became clear after a few days that more advanced methods of identifying bodies were necessary, especially for the two thousand tourists, mainly Europeans, who had been vacationing in Thailand at the time of the tsunami. Families wanted to bring the remains of their loved ones home, but without family members in Asia, the process of identification was far slower.

To assist the workers in Asia, hundreds of forensic specialists arrived from Europe and the United States. The forensic teams brought with them large shipping containers that contained generators. These could be used to refrigerate bodies, to protect them from the intense heat.

The teams carefully studied dental work so that it could be compared to dental records of those missing in Asia. They also snipped bits of skin, hair, or bone and sent the

specimens to labs in Bangkok or China for DNA analysis.
As the information began to filter in from the DNA work,
experts implanted in each body a tiny microchip the size of
a grain of rice. The microchip contained all the DNA information for that victim.

Even though a body's decomposition made visual identification impossible, the microchip provided accurate information that could be compared to family members'
DNA for a possible match. To make the process even

*Forensic teams in
Thailand collect DNA
to help identify badly
decomposed corpses.
Microchips encoded
with the DNA data
were then implanted in
the bodies.*

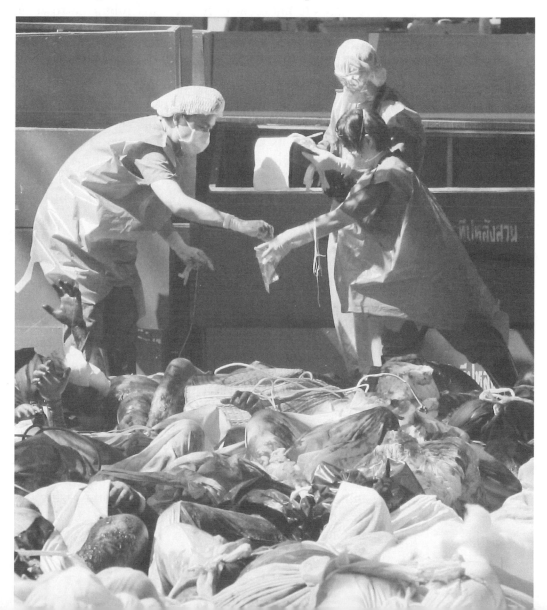

quicker, forensic specialists set up a twenty-four-hour DNA collection point at the Bangkok airport. Relatives of victims could give a sample of their DNA that could later be compared with any new bodies brought to the morgues.

"It's Harder than Rocket Science"

Besides dental and DNA analyses, forensic teams made note of any distinguishing marks, such as moles, tattoos, or scars. After assigning each body a number, workers posted on a Web site any characteristics that might narrow the search for relatives. Without limiting the search, say health workers, family members would have been forced to look at tens of thousands of decomposed bodies. The Web site got so much use that it crashed for hours at a time.

With more than three hundred forensic specialists, the identification system established in Thailand was the largest effort of its kind in history. They worked eighteen-hour shifts each day and said that the size of the job was overwhelming. One senior member of the American team of doctors had been involved with the aftermath of wars, terrorist attacks, and other disasters, but what he saw in Thailand was beyond anything he has ever experienced. "We've never been involved in anything of this magnitude," he says. "9/11 pales in comparison."[43]

Many workers said the hardest aspect of dealing with the victims of the tsunami was psychological. Seeing the weary families returning day after day without finding the person they were seeking was difficult, as is doing forensic work on so many young people. "This isn't rocket science," one worker says. "It's harder than rocket science because it's blended with human emotion."[44]

Nightmares and Uncertainty

Even with the large international forensic effort, however, identification of the bodies has been a slow process. In the meantime, the presence of so many dead and missing has taken a psychological toll on the survivors in the afflicted areas. One woman in Banda Aceh says that everywhere she walks, she sees bodies, and the expressions on their faces

Thai health workers bury bodies in a mass grave. Because of health concerns, most tsunami victims were given a swift and unceremonious burial.

both frighten and depress her. One of the most common effects is nightmares. Another woman in Thailand says her children cannot sleep more than an hour or two before nightmares about dead people wake them.

There is uncertainty, too, about who is dead, and psychologists warn that not knowing the fate of missing family members can be damaging for survivors. Every culture has traditions and rituals associated with death, which are comforting to grieving families. In Sri Lanka, for example, the body of the deceased is always displayed at the home several days before burial, so friends and neighbors can come by to light a candle and say a prayer. But so many bodies were buried or burned in the first hours after the tsunami that thousands of families were unsure about the fate of their missing loved ones. There were no bodies to display, no place to light candles for the dead.

Ghosts and Roaming Dead

Funerals are another tradition that had to be waived during the aftermath of the tsunami, especially in hard-hit areas where deaths numbered in the tens of thousands. Survivors throughout Southern Asia worried that because the dead were not given proper funerals, they would not go to the afterlife. Instead, their souls would be forced to roam the earth forever.

Fear of ghosts made it difficult for many people to return to their homes. One Indonesian woman returned to her home after 6 feet (1.83m) of water had receded only to find the bodies of a young woman and a baby that had floated into the house. She left because of the ghosts, she says. A Bangkok woman who occasionally visited Phuket, an area hard-hit by the tsunami, says she knows she will never return there. "The ghosts are a problem," she says matter-of-factly. "Thai people hate ghosts, and now Phuket is full of them. I won't go down there again."[45]

Workers retrieving bodies in Banda Aceh have thought a great deal about ghosts, too. They believe that the ghosts will leave once their bodies are recovered. One man, a fisherman, says that he is not afraid of them. "If a ghost comes to haunt me," he says, "I will just ask where his body is, so I can pick him up."[46]

People who have gone to Southern Asia to help in the tsunami's aftermath say that ghost stories abound in every affected region. Everyone knows someone who has seen a ghost or who has heard calls for help coming from the ocean in the middle of the night—and no one is there: "The grapevine is alive with ghost stories: the fisherman on Phi Phi Island who heard a large group of Westerners calling for help, but when he looked he saw nobody; the tuk-tuk [cab] driver who stopped for five tourists . . . then, when he looked behind him into the tuk-tuk, found no passengers."[47]

A Thai boy lights one of hundreds of candles on a beach in memory of a dead relative. Many Thais feared the ghosts of victims who were not given a proper burial.

To calm the fears of so many survivors in Thailand, Buddhist monks have been holding rituals to deal with the wandering spirits. The monks say simple prayers and burn incense or burn things that the spirits need in the next world, such as clothing or money. Many people say the ceremonies help. Putting the dead to rest in such ways, says one Thai psychologist, can be "a good healing method that is part of our culture."[48]

4

Grief, Guilt, and Pain

WHILE RESCUE WORKERS and forensic specialists dealt with the thousands of bodies, others concentrated on helping the survivors. Almost always, natural disasters are accompanied by outbreaks of disease, for many people are forced from their homes into refugee areas. Crowded, cramped conditions often overtax the sanitation systems available, and serious diseases usually follow.

Five Million People

The number of people made homeless by the tsunami was staggering, and public health officials were extremely worried. "Perhaps as many as five million people are not able to access what they need for living," said one doctor from the World Health Organization. "Either they cannot get water, or their sanitation is inadequate, or they cannot get food."[49]

There were 450 makeshift refugee camps in Sri Lanka alone, and with more than five hundred thousand people homeless there, the camps were filled beyond capacity. They were set up in schools, Buddhist temples, and wedding halls. When those structures were filled, "tent cities" were created outdoors. In Aceh province in Indonesia, there were so many homeless survivors that the government built semipermanent camps that could each accommodate twenty thousand people.

The most worrisome health threat was the lack of clean water. The salt water of the tsunami, combined with the heavy rains afterward, had contaminated every source of

Refugees in an Indonesian aid camp sift through donated items. Aid camps across Southern Asia struggled to accommodate the millions of people left homeless by the tsunamis.

drinking water in the affected regions. Rivers were flooded; wells had become poisoned with salt water or bacteria. Water treatment plants had been destroyed, too.

Health workers at the camps advised the refugees not to drink the water or even use it for bathing or washing clothes. But many survivors lived in remote areas and were not aware that the water sources had been contaminated. They continued to bathe in the rivers and even drink from the wells. One mother of four in Banda Aceh allowed her children to drink from a well, not understanding that the water was unclean. Her children all became ill. "It tasted funny," she recalled later. "Rather salty and strange."[50]

Fearing the Worst

Drinking contaminated water can result in a number of dangerous diseases that health experts say could more than double the number of deaths resulting from the tsunami. Cholera, for example, a highly lethal infection of the intestines, is caused by drinking contaminated water. The disease, which can result in death within hours if untreated, can cause a victim to lose more than 2 gallons (7.571l) of body fluid a day. Typhoid fever is another threat from contaminated water. It kills more than 12.5 million people annually, and flooded sewers greatly increase the risk of the disease. Diarrhea, too, is a threat even without natural disaster, especially to children. In 2003, more than 2.2 million people—most of them under the age of twelve—died from diarrhea.

Health officials insisted that the best way to fight outbreaks of these diseases was clean water. In some instances, the ruined roads made it impossible to get enough tanks of clean water to those who needed it. Instead, authorities recommended that health workers begin a water purification process called flocculation. First, a harmless chemical solution is added to water that causes dirt in the water to form clusters, so it can be easily filtered. Then a very small amount of chlorine bleach is added—several

A U.S. Navy soldier tests water samples taken from Banda Aceh. Experts worried that contaminated water would lead to outbreaks of disease in the tsunami's aftermath.

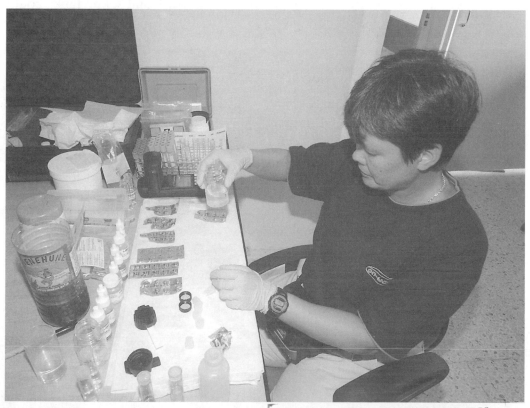

SWAMPSCOTT PUBLIC LIBRARY
Swampscott, Massachusetts 01907-1996

drops for a quart of water. Within a half hour, the bleach kills almost all of the bacteria, making the water safe to drink.

It is a painstaking process, and because of the chemical additive, an expensive one. However, experts say that it was absolutely critical to provide clean drinking water as quickly as possible. Health workers say that the heat and scarcity of water had made some people so thirsty they had begun to drink sewer water, even knowing it would surely make them ill.

Lack of Sanitation

Sri Lankan children walk through filthy floodwater. Lack of adequate sanitation was a tremendous concern to health workers.

In addition to the scarcity of clean water, the lack of adequate sanitation was a worry to health workers. Sewer systems had been ruined by the tsunami, and septic tanks and latrines were filled with a combination of salt water and rainwater. Again, because of the washed-out roads, the trucks that could pump out latrines and septic tanks could not get through.

At the refugee camps, the situation was especially intense. In Aceh province in Indonesia, twenty-one large camps had to be relocated to higher ground when heavy rains washed out all their toilet facilities. The ground was so saturated that, until the ground dried, it was impossible to dig more latrines for the refugees.

Because dangerous diseases spread quickly by contact with fecal matter from an infected person, doctors were initially concerned that the lack of sanitation in the camps could create havoc from a single case of cholera or diarrhea. Their worry was compounded by deteriorating conditions. "Rain and overcrowding is making a bad situation worse," one UNICEF official said in the weeks just after the tsunami. "Emergency facilities are being over-stretched and construction of new toilets is not keeping up with the demand. Conditions are becoming miserable for families, leaving them little defense against disease."[51]

"No One Seems to Have Any Experience"

While public health officials were ramping up their efforts to avoid epidemics by correcting the problems with water and sanitation, doctors were desperately trying to save the lives of people who had been injured in the tsunami. Not surprisingly, doctors in Indonesia, Sri Lanka, and India were overwhelmed, not only by the numbers of wounded, but by the nature of their injuries.

Many people had inhaled a great deal of salt water as they tried to outrun or swim through the waves. Salt water is dangerous, because it not only damages tender lung tissue, but can lead to heart failure in many cases. One doctor was frustrated because he had no idea how to treat these patients and could find little information on the subject. "No one seems to have any experience with this," he says. "We can't find anything, not even on the Internet."[52]

By far the most common injuries were infections, and these, too, were frustrating for doctors. They were seeing grossly infected arms and legs, wounds that in normal situations could have been healed with a little antiseptic cream and a clean bandage. Instead, the wounds festered and became so infected that doctors often had little choice but to amputate the limb.

"Rip-Roaring" Infections

One reason for the problem is that it took far longer than usual for the injured to find doctors. The chaos of relocation, especially in areas that did not have many doctors, kept many of the injured from getting emergency care. "To some extent," a doctor in Banda Aceh said, "a process of natural selection has occurred. People with no treatment at all are already dead."[53]

The other reason for the number of life-threatening infections was the presence of so much stagnant water. Many survivors were pelted by debris as they fled the waves—jagged shards of glass, bits of wood, and pieces of corrugated tin. Their cuts quickly became infected because it was simply impossible to avoid contact with the water, say doctors. The water contained bacteria of all kinds, including those from animal and human waste. "A couple of drops of this putrid water gives these people rip-roaring pneumonia and lacerations that get horrendously infected," says one doctor. "The surgical cases have become more complicated because the infections are becoming more spectacular."[54]

A final grim reason for the lack of emergency care was that so many doctors and nurses were killed in the tsunami or had family members who had been killed. One doctor from Sumatra says that in his hospital, many colleagues were too distracted by their own losses to work. "Our hospital was crippled," he says. "Most of our doctors were too traumatized to work, or left to look for loved ones missing after the tsunami."[55]

Guilt over Lost Children

It was not only the physical problems of the survivors that needed attention, however. Many relief workers reported widespread psychological problems affecting a great many of the people who survived the tsunami. One trauma expert notes that in places like Banda Aceh, which lost more than

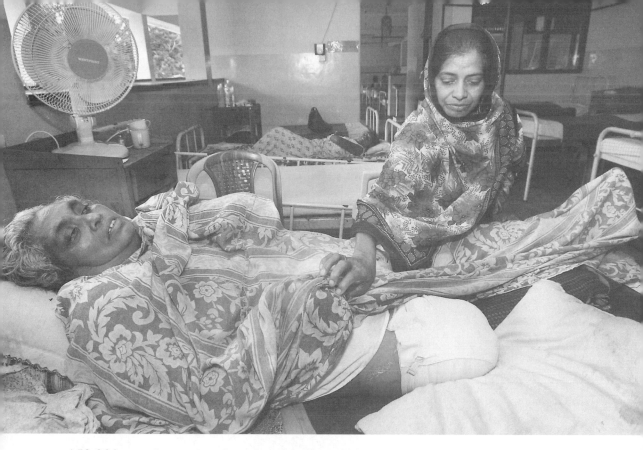

150,000 people, trauma is a formidable problem. "Indonesia has only a tiny number of people trained to give the sort of psychological counseling that might help," he says. "Tens of thousands of people, therefore, may suffer permanent mental harm."[56]

A Sri Lankan woman cares for her sister, who lost ten family members and her right leg as a result of the tsunami.

Many were overwhelmed by feelings of guilt—especially parents whose children were killed. Experts believe that between one-third and one-half of the victims of the tsunami were children. A reporter in Sri Lanka walked through a village where fishermen were searching for survivors. When anyone passed, the men held up two, three, or more fingers, to indicate how many children they had lost.

Had the waves arrived on a weekday, many children in Thailand, Sri Lanka, and Indonesia would have been further inland, at school. But because it was Sunday, most children were home or with their mothers at the fish markets, close to the shore. Because they thought the loud roar they heard was an airplane, many mothers did not react quickly enough. By the time they realized what was actually occurring, they had lost valuable time.

They grabbed their children, but two hands were sometimes not enough. One Indian woman grabbed two of her four children, yelling to the older ones to hold on to their baby brothers' hands, but the waves were simply too strong. Another saved two of her children, but lost her grip on a third child. Afterwards, she sobbed, "I could not hold three."[57]

"I Killed the Children"

The tremendous guilt, say counselors, is understandable, for the grieving parents are tormented by the idea that they failed to do what parents are supposed to do—protect their children. Relief workers in the refugee camps say that "if only" is one of the phrases heard most often among parents whose children did not survive.

In Sri Lanka, one mother is haunted by her decision to run a short errand, just a minute from her oceanfront home.

An Indonesian survivor searches for relatives among piles of children's bodies. Many parents who lost children in the tsunami were racked with feelings of guilt.

She left her six-year-old and six-month-old sleeping; seconds before she returned, the wave hit. Her children were drowned. She cannot speak because she is so sad, explains one observer, but instead "her eyes tear and she waves her hand in front of her heart in small, frantic circles."[58]

Another mother, Ms. Thanaranjani, cannot remember what happened—she was carrying her four-year-old daughter while running next to her eight-year-old, and when the older daughter was washed away, the woman blacked out. Her husband later found the bodies of both daughters. "I feel that I should have died with the kids," Ms. Thanaranjani says. "People blame me. They said I could have saved at least one."[59]

A grandmother, Chinnapillai, is tormented because she urged her daughter to bring her two young children to live near her, by the ocean. Chinnapillai says that she had taken her two grandchildren to the shore to watch the fishermen bring their boats in when the waves suddenly came. She grabbed their hands, but the powerful waves separated them. Sobbing, she says, "I killed the children."[60]

Children Alone

While a large percentage of the victims of the tsunami were children, a great many adults also perished. The result is thousands of children throughout Southern Asia whose lives have been upended. Either they have lost their families, or they have not been able to find them. And while the word *orphan* is not a common one in Indonesia, since extended family is almost always there to help, it has been used a great deal since December 26, 2004. In Aceh province alone, thirty-five thousand children are thought to have lost both parents.

The refugee camps filled early with children who were so frightened that they did not speak to anyone. Many showed signs of depression by sleeping or refusing to interact with anyone else. One boy at a camp in Sri Lanka cried for days while clinging to the only thing he had of his mother's—a torn piece of fabric from her dress. A little girl said she did not remember her own name.

Photos of children looking to be reunited with their parents cover the wall of a refugee camp in Indonesia.

Counselors say that trauma is natural during such a monstrous time, but that they worried children did not seem to rally even weeks after the event. A UNICEF spokesman, Martin Dawes, says that in Sri Lanka many children were "in a state of denial."[61] Even after seeing their mothers drown, many children still believed their mothers would return for them. Many were not eating and seemed to have simply given up.

"I Embraced Them"

Fourteen-year-old Andrian lost twenty-six members of his extended family, including both parents and all of his siblings. In addition, his friends from his neighborhood and from school were killed. But while his life will be drastically changed, counselors insist that he was luckier than many children. He will be raised by four uncles, whose wives were killed by the tsunami, and an eighty-year-old grandfather. "We will push him through school," says one uncle, "and make sure he makes it."[62]

Some children have been taken in by rescuers, too. Chaidir Syamsul, an architect in Aceh province, found three disoriented children in the hours after the tsunami. He took them to a refugee camp where his wife and four children had fled. Although two of the children were reunited with relatives at the camp, the twelve-year-old boy (named Iqbal) had no one and was immediately invited to join the Syamsul family.

"I called [the three children], I embraced them," Syamsul explains, "and I took them away to a higher place. . . . I feel like [Iqbal] is my own son. How much love I give to my own son, I will give to him."[63]

Not So Lucky

But other children were not so lucky. Many were taken to temporary orphanages while relief workers tried to locate missing parents. Some children were brought in by a parent —usually a father—who could no longer take care of a child. Some men who lost their wives were overwhelmed by the idea of raising a small child, and because many of them have also had their fishing boats destroyed, they have no way of making a living.

One little boy was dropped off by his father at an orphanage in India right after the tsunami hit. He was confused, workers say, because he assumed his father would return for him. "He doesn't come to visit," says the boy. "He promised to come back and get me."[64]

In the first month after the tsunami, in one small orphanage in India, ninety-nine children waited. Half of them lost both mother and father, while the rest were dropped off by a father. One warden said that some of the children probably had relatives, but in many cases, the relatives were unwilling to take on another child. "Even if their relatives had the money to care for them," he said, "they don't wish it. The families may have up to eight children of their own. Taking these children would be too much."[65]

Trafficking Children

There was a more serious threat to the orphans of the tsunami, however. Within forty-eight hours of the disaster,

These Indian orphans of the tsunami were placed in a state-run home. Some less-fortunate orphans were kidnapped by child traffickers and sold into slavery.

child protection workers in Indonesia learned that human traffickers were preying on child refugees in Aceh province. The traffickers, who have been a dangerous problem for years in Indonesia, take or buy children and sell them either as forced laborers or as sex workers in brothels throughout Southern Asia.

Birgithe Lund-Henriksen, chief of the child protection unit for UNICEF in Southeast Asia, says that she received a copy of a message that said: "300 orphans, age 3 to 10 years, from Aceh for adoption. All paperwork will be taken care of. No fee. Please state age and sex of child required."[66]

The chaos that ensued after the tsunami made the situation easy for traffickers to abduct young children, for there were so many who had no adults supervising them. In one Sumatran village, an observer counted more than seven hundred young children who were unaccompanied. Says one child welfare worker, "It's a perfect opportunity for these guys to move in."[67]

In response to the threat, the Indonesian government banned any child from leaving the country unless the accompanying adults could document that they were the parents or guardians. The ban also applied to well-meaning foreigners who hoped that they could adopt an orphaned child. Many Indonesian people were adamant that it would be wrong to allow orphaned children to leave Indonesia. "The children left without parents must be in their communities, and their culture," explains a social service official. "That's our principle."[68]

Child psychologists agreed. The youngest survivors of the tsunami were suffering a great deal of emotional pain. The trauma of the disaster and the horror of losing their family and home were terrible enough, but to lose their culture and everything that is familiar would have been unspeakable. "The children have been through a massive shock," says one international relief worker. "We shouldn't make life even harder by uprooting them."[69]

5

The World Responds

AS THE RELIEF WORKERS in Southern Asia were frantically dealing with the aftereffects of the tsunami, the rest of the world was just learning about what had occurred. Interestingly, as CNN and other major news networks throughout the world scrambled to the affected regions to offer the first pictures and accounts of the tragedy, they quickly realized that they had been beaten—by tourists.

"Just Had a Big Tidal Wave Hit"

Images of the waves, home videotape of groups of people literally being washed away, and personal narratives about the tsunami—all of these were being sent home via cell phones, computers, and video cameras. As these devices have become smaller and more affordable, they allow any vacationer with a video camera or an Internet connection to be a reporter. And there is no better proof of that than what occurred within moments of the tsunami.

Not surprisingly, some of the fast communications were messages of reassurance. Sam Nicols, who was rock climbing in Thailand, used text messaging on his cell phone to tell his father in Oregon that he was unharmed. "Just had a big tidal wave hit," the first message read. "I am not injured but lost some climbing gear, my camera. . . . Please tell family am safe."[70]

Another key use of the technology was to help people throughout the world search for the missing. Within hours of the tsunami, chat rooms on the Internet, set up by travel agencies, relief organizations, the International Red Cross,

and other groups, were allowing people to post names and descriptions of their missing friends and relatives. One editor of an online journal says that the technology was an amazing leap beyond what had been possible in years past in such a disaster. "Anyone in the world can put up a bulletin board, and anyone else can search it and find a name," she says. "That's a miracle. The same tools we use to find the best buys on Amazon come into play when we're trying to find out who's alive and who's dead."[71]

This still shot of a tidal wave hitting a Thai beach is from video shot by an amateur. Soon after the disaster, such dramatic footage was compiled on DVD and sold (inset).

"We Would Have Gone On to the Super Bowl"

But the most valuable result of the use of cell phones, the Internet, and video cameras by tourists was that it made the event seem far more immediate to the world. "It was close to home," says one girl who watched video taken by a vacationer in Thailand:

> It was on the news—they played it constantly the first day or two after the tsunami hit.
>
> It was like you could see the wave, this big blue wall of water. And people were running—it was shaky, like you'd expect. I'm watching this, and it made me tremble—because it wasn't a movie. It was shaky, and you realize as you're watching this thing that those little kids in their bathing suits are going to die. I can't tell you how much that affected me. I felt like that could have been me, or my sister, or whoever, you know? It really was terrifying in a personal way.[72]

Media expert Ben Bagdikian agrees, saying that the empathy people feel by experiencing an event through such personal technology is dramatic in ways that regular news reporting is not. He says that if the tsunami had struck twenty years ago, "we would have reported it, it would have been seen as a huge disaster, and we would have gone on to the Super Bowl."[73] Instead, however, the closeness of the tragedy is far more pronounced, and people are more interested in following the story. "I wanted to know right off, what can I do," says Pam, who watched coverage of the tsunami for hours each day. "Everyone they interviewed had a different story to tell, and when they'd interview people who were searching for a missing child, I was in tears, too. I'm not rich—I'm usually pretty broke before payday, but I sent in fifty dollars to the Red Cross, and my roommate did, too. I don't know how anyone could watch and not want to help."[74]

"An Outpouring of International Assistance"

As the coverage continued and the death toll from Southern Asia continued to skyrocket, the governments of the world pledged their assistance in aiding and rebuilding the region. Within seventy-two hours, governments around the world had pledged more than $4 billion of aid for tsunami relief.

The United States offered use of its military planes and ships to deliver aid, as well as $350 million in cash. The largest donation was that of Australia, which pledged $815 million. The next-highest pledges were those of Germany ($660 million) and Japan ($500 million). While Norway's donation of $180 million was quite a bit less than others, it was the largest per capita offering, at $39 per citizen.

Jan Egeland, the United Nation's emergency relief coordinator, was heartened at the quick response of the international community. He says that he had "never, ever seen such an outpouring of international assistance in any international disaster, ever."[75]

A Mexican rescue team flies to Thailand after the tsunami. Aid teams across the world responded immediately to the disaster.

No Frozen Croissants

But governmental donations were just part of the world-wide effort to help Southern Asia. Millions of people made private donations, too. To speed up the process, President George W. Bush asked former presidents Bill Clinton and George H.W. Bush to head a joint effort to drum up private donations through charities already existing, such as the International Red Cross, CARE, and UNICEF.

Clinton insisted that the contributions of thousands or millions of dollars were not the only ones that were valuable. Individual small donations, when combined, would also help the people of Southern Asia. "I want people here at home in America and throughout the world," he announced, "to know that if you only have a dollar, $5, $10 to give—if a million of you do, that you'll make a huge difference."[76]

Many charities agreed, and they also asked that people make cash donations, rather than pledge food or clothing for

Bill Clinton poses with sailors aboard a ship bound for Southern Asian disaster sites. Clinton and George H.W. Bush headed U.S. aid efforts.

the refugees. Besides being very expensive to ship overseas, such items are often not what is needed. A spokesperson for Oxfam, a large international relief organization, says that even though people mean well, history has shown that donations of food and other items are often inappropriate. In 1991, after 139,000 people were killed in a Bangladesh cyclone, he says, "the French were sending frozen croissants and frozen dinners, and there was an American shipment of peanut butter. No one in Bangladesh really knew what it was, and people ended up feeding it to their animals."[77]

Creative Giving

In addition to using the Internet to donate money to charities, people found other ways to help. Moved by the large number of children who were victims of the tsunami, young people found ways to give, too. In Chicago, a group of teens got pledges from area grocery stores and sold hot dogs and soda at high school games, giving all the proceeds to CARE. Boy Scouts, Girl Scouts, and church youth groups solicited donations in their neighborhoods for children's relief agencies. One eighth-grade class in Wenatchee, Washington, donated all the money they had saved for their class trip to Canada to the Red Cross instead.

Many entertainers around the world offered to hold benefit concerts for charity. Madonna, Eric Clapton, John Mayer, and others performed in an event on January 15, 2005, called "Tsunami Aid: A Concert of Hope." In Wales, almost sixty-five thousand rock and blues fans attended an all-star concert on January 22, 2005, raising almost $2 million. Finally, stars like Bono, Norah Jones, Tim McGraw, Stevie Wonder, and Steven Tyler performed "Across the Universe," a song written by John Lennon and Paul McCartney. For ninety-nine cents, fans could download the song on a Web site, and all proceeds went to charities helping the tsunami victims.

Some of the most creative giving by private citizens involved the "adoption" of a village destroyed by the tsunami. In the United States, certain radio stations raised money to provide aid to particular villages. For example,

Many musical artists staged tsunami relief concerts worldwide. Barenaked Ladies, a popular rock group, is shown here performing at a relief concert in Canada.

several stations in Minneapolis got together to adopt Ban Sai Khao Moo, a small fishing village in Thailand. "By describing real people in a place, and talking about what those people do for a living, how they've been affected by the tsunami, that makes it so real to me," says one college student. "When I give my donation, I feel like I know exactly where it's going. I think this is the best idea of all—it's so much more personal than just handing over your money to a big fund. I like that I'm helping the people of Ban Sai Khao Moo—maybe I'll visit someday!"[78]

In America's Best Interest

While many people worked to raise money for the stricken region, it was also necessary to see that supplies such as medicine, food, and water got to the survivors quickly. This was a job that the United States took on, largely because of the strength and size of its military.

The U.S. Navy sent the *USS Abraham Lincoln*, a large aircraft carrier, along with twenty-one other ships and ninety aircraft—with a total of almost fourteen thousand crew members—to the waters off Indonesia, Thailand, and Sri Lanka. The large military deployment cost the Pentagon about $5.6 million per day, but many U.S. officials felt that it was an important opportunity for the United States to be seen in the role of humanitarian.

Secretary of State Colin Powell toured the affected areas and met with officials in Indonesia, the most populous Muslim nation. He insisted that even though the United States was in the process of fighting terrorism among some Islamic groups, the people of Indonesia should understand that Americans do not look on Muslims as enemies. "America is not an anti-Islam, anti-Muslim nation," he said. "America is a diverse society where we respect all religions. And I hope that as a result of our efforts, as a result of our helicopter pilots being seen by the citizens of Indonesia helping them, that value system of ours will be reinforced."[79]

"Nonstop from Dawn Until Sunset"

By January 1, four full days after the tsunami hit, the first U.S. contingent was ready to start bringing supplies ashore. Seahawk helicopters began ferrying loads of supplies from the *Lincoln* to some of the hardest-hit villages in Aceh, close to the quake's epicenter. Helicopter crews dropped off boxes of power bars, strawberry yogurt, and water to the gathering crowds of people and returned to the ship for another load.

Other nations were sending planes loaded with supplies, too, but they were having trouble getting into Aceh. The airport consists of only one small airstrip, which could not handle the number of planes arriving. On January 1, the airport closed for hours when a 737, filled with medical workers and supplies, tried to land and hit a water buffalo. It took hours before the damaged plane could be moved off the runway to allow other planes to land.

But once the supplies arrived at Aceh airport, there was nowhere for them to go. Many trucks lay on their sides, damaged by the waves. There were no gasoline reserves at the airport, and even if someone could get a truck running, the roads and bridges connecting the airport with the surrounding regions had been washed away. It was clear that the helicopters would be the only way supplies could be distributed from the airport.

Navy officials reported that the Seahawks were working between thirteen and eighteen missions a day at first, just to get emergency aid out. As each helicopter returned from its last mission of the day, maintenance crews immediately descended on it, making sure it was safe and ready to begin early the next day. "We're going nonstop from dawn until sunset," said the executive officer of the *Lincoln*. "Then the commanders meet, talk about what we've learned that day, and map out what needs to be done tomorrow."[80]

Many members of the Seahawk crews were stunned by the enormous need of the survivors. Desperate people

A U.S. Navy hospital ship steams alongside the USS Abraham Lincoln *en route to Indonesia. Twenty-one American ships provided aid.*

rushed toward the helicopters, even before they landed, stretching out their arms for water or a little food. During the first emergency missions, the crowds sometimes became unruly, but as people understood that more deliveries would come, they became more patient.

Though crew members admitted that they were tired from the long days, they also said that they were glad to be part of the relief effort. "A lot of these people are so weak—they hadn't eaten for days," one lieutenant observed. "It feels like we're really doing something to help. The people are so grateful—they put their hands over their hearts, to thank us. You realize that without [the food and water we're bringing them], many of them wouldn't last long."[81]

A Changed Landscape

In addition to the great number of missions each day, the helicopter crews struggled with other problems, too. One was the difficulty of navigation. So much of the coastal areas had been destroyed by the tsunami that maps of the

Tsunami victims rush to grab food supplies delivered by a U.S. Navy helicopter. Only helicopters were able to reach remote disaster sites.

area were virtually useless, for nothing looked the same to the pilots. In these instances, the helicopter crews tried to get help from people, but the language barrier became a frustration.

"We land in villages and we can't understand what they're telling us," said one officer. "People tell us there's a village six kilometers [3.8 miles] away that needs food, and then we go out looking for it and can't find it, and we have to go back two or three times looking for it." The only thing they could do, he said, was to keep searching, "We try and fly different routes each day to find villages we're missing."[82] He added that the only reason his crew was able to find a remote village that day was because they had created a signal in a nearby field using white stones.

Tiger Trouble

Potentially more serious was the problem of civil unrest that was ongoing in two of the affected regions. Sri Lanka, where an estimated thirty-eight thousand people died in the tsunami, has been engaged in a civil war since the 1980s. A mostly Hindu rebel group known as the Tamil Tigers has been waging a guerrilla war against the Sri Lankan government, which is predominantly Buddhist.

The presence of the U.S. military in Sri Lanka was worrisome to Tamil officials. Since 1997, the United States has included the Tamil Tigers on a list of terrorist organizations because they have targeted civilians in suicide bombings. After the tsunami, Tamil officials were nervous about allowing troops of any nation, including Sri Lanka and the United States, into their territory.

But officials in the Bush administration assured Tamil leaders that soldiers were there to deliver and distribute aid, nothing more. Giving aid to the victims in no way changed the fact that the United States still condemned the Tigers' methods. Says one U.S. administrator, "[W]e . . . need to make it clear to them what we are doing, so they don't mistake our presence there as anything more than humanitarian."[83] Other than exchanges of angry words between government and Tamil officials, however, international

relief workers and visiting troops were able to do their work without incident.

Civil Strife in Aceh Province

The civil unrest in Indonesia was potentially an even more dangerous situation. The people in Aceh province have been fighting for their independence for more than one hundred years—first against the Dutch, then the Japanese, and now against the Indonesian government. Aceh's impoverished citizens feel that they are being used by the Indonesians, who take the province's gas and oil reserves and sell them, but never share the profits with the residents.

The Indonesian government has sent the national army to be a presence in Aceh, and there have been many instances of torture and execution of rebels by soldiers. On the other hand, members of the Aceh resistance have fought back, targeting people they believe are collaborating with

Tamil Tiger rebels stand guard during a funeral in Sri Lanka. Civil strife in Sri Lanka continued despite the tsunami disaster.

the government. Since 1990, more than 100,000 people have died in the civil war in Aceh.

Although there was no doubt that it was necessary to send relief workers into Aceh—it was the hardest hit of any region—the Indonesian government restricted the movement of all humanitarian workers. Many relief agencies felt that the restrictions were imposed because Indonesia did not want interference in the way it is handling the unrest. Some raised a more serious charge: that the Indonesian military was not particularly interested in whether the Aceh rebels got help or not.

"A Political Minefield"

Relief workers from around the world objected to the government's restrictions, saying that the government-imposed 6:00 P.M. curfew and the requirement that all aid workers must travel with armed military escorts were hurting those who needed help.

Relief workers at this multinational aid station in Aceh, Indonesia, were forced to contend with political unrest as they sought to provide aid to tsunami victims.

But the Indonesian government stood firm, insisting that it could not guarantee the safety of relief workers otherwise —a claim the rebels dismissed immediately. "Our mothers, our wives, our children are victims from this tragedy," says one leader of the insurgency. "We would never ambush any convoy with aid for them."[84]

The presence of the U.S. military in Aceh was a source of concern for some Indonesian officials, too. They worried that the United States may have wanted to assist the rebels, and, if that happened, there would be a great deal of tension between the two nations. Sidney Jones of the International Crisis Group, which monitors conflicts throughout the world, says that U.S. soldiers in Indonesia were placed in a very sticky situation: "I think they're walking into a political minefield."[85]

The inhabitants of Aceh province were not worried about the presence of foreign troops, however. One young man, a tailor, who after three weeks was still living under a plastic sheet in a refugee camp with forty-five relatives, was glad that the U.S. soldiers were there, for he believed that they would make sure that aid was distributed fairly— something the Indonesian troops would not. "If [the foreign troops] leave," he says simply, "we will starve."[86]

6

An Uncertain Future

THE INITIAL RESPONSE of the international community
—sending emergency rations of food, medicine, and water—
was a critical first step for Southern Asia. However, it was
quickly obvious that the region would need long-term assistance, not tons more of emergency aid. In February, less
than two months after the disaster, Sri Lankan officials announced that survivors in refugee camps and elsewhere
had more supplies than they needed.

So that the perishable items did not go to waste, officials
said, they decided to divert the supplies to the elderly and
centers for disabled children. And while there was no question that the emergency aid had been a lifesaver for the victims, officials confided that what they really needed was
help rebuilding homes. That sentiment was echoed by others, too. Psychologically and economically, it was important for the people of the area to get to work, to rebuild
what was destroyed, and to get on with their lives.

Rebuilding

Disaster relief experts agree wholeheartedly. An administrator of Oxfam stressed that the task of rebuilding will
take years. The easy part, he says, is pledging money for
emergency relief, but after the first few weeks, that phase
is over. It is the next phase that requires a commitment.
"People think, when you've got the bodies off the beach,
the job is over," he says. "But the job has just begun."[87]

Repairing the damage in Southern Asia, experts say, will
be on a giant scale, for it is the systems—the infrastructure

of the region—that must be rebuilt. With millions of people displaced, with workers unemployed, with factories and farmland ruined, with schools closed, the rebuilding is going to take a great deal of money and time. That is why it will be critical for governments who have pledged millions of dollars—or hundreds of millions—to honor those pledges. Surprisingly, that has not been the case in past disasters.

In 2003, for example, when an earthquake devastated part of southeastern Iran, the international community

U.S. relief workers in Sri Lanka help local residents begin the process of rebuilding their homes and lives. The task will take years.

pledged more than $1 billion to help Iran rebuild. How-
ever, only $17.5 million was ever sent. The same thing
happened in 1998, when Hurricane Mitch struck Honduras
and Nicaragua. Those nations received less than one-third
of the aid they had been promised.

One human rights worker says that pledges are often
broken because of disinterest:

> People—governments, private citizens, whatever—get fired
> up to help after a disaster. They want to help when they see
> the pictures of the hungry kids crying. Who wouldn't? But
> two or three weeks later, [the disaster] is off the front page,
> and we're on to something else. The world has turned, and
> new things are happening, so the money doesn't get sent—or
> at least not all of it does.

> It should be different—everyone says that it's the rebuilding
> that's the most valuable in the long run. But rebuilding—or de-
> velopment, as it's called in budgets—just isn't as interesting as
> emergency relief. Compared to getting food to starving kids,
> building a road or staffing a clinic or getting new fishing equip-
> ment to replace the ruined stuff seems boring, even though, in
> the long run, that road or that clinic or the new fishing equip-
> ment may be critically important to the growth of that area.[88]

"Putting Plaster on the Wound"

One of the key elements in the wise use of aid, agree many
experts, is focusing on the future of the region. Even if all
the funds pledged do get sent, United Nations (UN) official
Jan Egeland worries that they will not be used wisely.
Though well-meaning, the international community often
wastes a great deal of money earmarking funds for emergency relief rather than prevention. As a result, says Egeland, the world spends its money on short-term solutions.
"I am acutely aware of how much money is being spent on
being fire brigades, us putting plaster on the wound," he
says, "and too little on preventing the devastation and suffering in the first place."[89]

Egeland speaks from experience. In 2000, Mozambique
feared that it was vulnerable to disaster from flooding and
requested $2.7 million in prevention aid from the interna-
tional community. The world gave only half that amount.

Ironically, however, when a flood devastated the region a few months later, the nations of the world gladly donated $200 million!

Disaster experts say that this is what they hope to avoid in Southern Asia. There are a number of things that can be done to lessen the impact of future earthquakes and tsunamis. The first priority, many agreed, was a tsunami warning system in the Indian Ocean.

A Model in the Pacific Ocean

Geologists believe that the warning system used currently in the Pacific Ocean is a fine example of the technology that is available. It consists of a number of elements, the first of which are seismic sensors. There are 150 of these placed throughout the Pacific. They scan for any undersea tremors that could be the beginning of an underwater earthquake—the cause of most tsunamis.

Above the water are tide monitors, which measure variances in the level of the sea. If scientists suspect that a strong earthquake has occurred below the water, they can check whether the monitors show any dramatic changes in water level. Wave buoys, or "tsunameters," are the most expensive part of the system. They are undersea instruments that pick up minute changes in water pressure—another sign of a tsunami. If the tsunameters register a change, they pass on the data to a buoy above water, which transmits the information to a satellite, which is monitored by technicians.

If information from the sensors indicates that a tsunami is likely, scientists in the Pacific have established a network to warn the governments of any nations that could be affected. There is also a system by which the public is alerted by sirens or by emergency radio and television updates. Experts estimate that the death count in Southern Asia could have been lowered considerably had such a system been in place. It is too late for the victims of this disaster, says UN specialist Salvano Briceno, but he vowed that the Indian Ocean system would be set up soon. "In the matter of a year, at latest eighteen months," he promised in a January

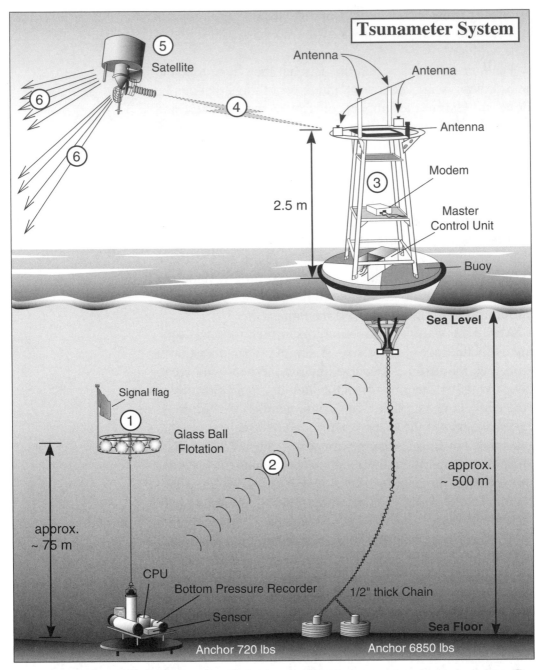

If a tsunameter ① registers a change in water pressure, it can pass on the data ② to a buoy above water ③. In turn, the data is transmitted ④ from the buoy to a satellite in space ⑤. The satellite can then send that same data ⑥ to scientists at several tsunami warning centers around the Pacific Ocean.

21, 2005, news conference, "there should be a basic re-
gional capacity on tsunami early warning."[90]

"Half of Them Go Down to the Beach"

While the promise of a warning system pleases the nations
on the Indian Ocean, seismologists warn that the equipment is not a cure-all. Training and experience are necessary so data can be evaluated and measured accurately.
Even more important, says one Hawaii-based expert, the
network set up to alert the right people must be in place if
the system is to work. "Unless you have a good system for
spreading an authentic warning and getting a quick response, the technology is not going to help you much," he
advises. "You have to have your emergency management
people ready and the public ready to respond."[91]

The public, too, has to have some idea of the seriousness
of an alert. Just as some people in the Great Plains states will
walk outside to catch a glimpse of a coming tornado, many
people do not understand the danger of exposure to a
tsunami. "If all you do is phone the local police station, they
don't know what to do," says an Australian tsunami expert.
"And in fact, one of the problems is that if you tell untrained
people, 'Look, there's a tsunami coming,' half of them go
down to the beach to see what a tsunami looks like."[92]

The public-alert system would be difficult to install in
some areas, especially in nontourist regions, such as Indonesia. Some experts worry that so many families of fishermen who live near the coast and are the most vulnerable
lack television and radio. These families would depend almost totally on sirens for warning. That will be a challenge
that the technology experts need to address.

Restoring the Economy

While an early warning system will be valuable, there are
still enormous hurdles ahead for the affected nations of
Southern Asia. One of the most critical is the damaged
economies of the region. "Until we get our economy going," says one man from Thailand, "we'll be dependent on
others for our well-being, and none of us wants that."[93]

Empty beach chairs stand as mute testimony to the lack of tourists in tsunami-ravaged areas. Most of the stricken nations depend on tourism as their principal industry.

In several nations affected by the tsunami—Thailand, Sri Lanka, and the Maldives (islands 400 miles [643.74km] southwest of Sri Lanka)—tourism is one of the most important pieces of their economy. In 2004, tourism-related business accounted for more than $100 billion. In the Maldives, it usually represents 80 percent of the economy.

But the popular restaurants and hotels of the region lie on the coasts, and as a result, many were destroyed. In Sri Lanka alone, the tsunami reduced two-thirds of its hotels to rubble. However, some hotels in all of these areas were not damaged, and in Thailand and the Maldives, beaches were among the first areas to be cleared. Hotel and resort owners whose property was intact hoped that people who had made vacation plans would still arrive. After the natural disaster, they had no wish to endure an economic one.

The news was not good, however. People around the world saw television coverage of the rows of body bags, the demolished buildings, and the refugee camps. Most who had made reservations canceled quickly. One German travel agent had fifteen hundred customers who had made plans to visit Thailand or Sri Lanka cancel their trips.

Tempting Vacationers

In Southern Asia, those in the tourism industry begged travel agents around the world to get the word out that there were many places unaffected by the disaster. The weather was good, the beaches were clear. One travel agent explained to his customers that there were still beautiful hotels that had been untouched by the waves.

Many Southern Asian tourist sites were unaffected by the tsunami and badly need visitors to help their flagging economies.

A French travel agent also urged her customers to reconsider their decision to cancel their plans and to think of a vacation in Thailand as assisting the victims of the tsunami. "There is no better way to help the people of this region," she said, "than to go on a holiday here."[94]

Some businesses offered deals to make a Southern Asian vacation more tempting. A Thai airline offered free tickets to travelers who used them within a month of the disaster. In all, they gave out 10,000 free tickets to Phuket, a popular resort area. "Through this offer, we estimate that we will bring at least 30,000 tourists to Phuket," says an airline representative. "We think this will be more encouraging than simply donating money."[95]

The Fishing Industry

Fishing is another industry hurt by the disaster. Along the islands and coasts of the Indian Ocean, hundreds of thousands of people are supported by the fishing industry. Much of their catch is bought by markets in Japan, Australia, and New Zealand. But for a number of reasons, after the tsunami, much of the fishing industry came to a halt.

The most obvious reason, of course, was the destruction of fishing boats, the specially woven fishing nets, and even the piers and docks along the coast. It is estimated that more than fifteen thousand fishing boats of every size were lost throughout the region during the tsunami. Many fishermen who wished to return to work could not begin to think about it until they had enough money to build new boats or docks or buy the material to have a new net made. "I need my boat," explains Poey Dee, a Thai fisherman. "If I get that, I can make it. Fishing is my job, my life, and the life of this village."[96]

While many shared Poey Dee's determination to resume fishing, others were reluctant to return to the sea. Although it is little talked about, this reluctance is another reason why the fishing industry is on hold in Southern Asia. The tsunami frightened people in a way that they had never experienced. Suddenly, the sustaining ocean that had always been a source of beauty and a place to fish had become an

Boats and docks damaged by the tsunami have brought the vital Southern Asian fishing industry to a near standstill.

unpredictable enemy that the fishermen cannot forgive. "Since my childhood, I've known nothing more closely than the sea," says one young man who lost his entire family. "Now I hate it."[97]

Many fishermen agreed, saying that they were more inclined to move from the coast, to find another type of work if possible, than to return to the sea. One man said that when he looked out at the ocean, he saw a cemetery instead.

Another worried that even if he began fishing again, there may be no one to buy the fish. Some markets had expressed concern about buying fish caught in areas where there were so many missing human corpses.

"I'm Afraid, But I Have to Do It"

Trauma experts say that survivors of the tsunami, in addition to having lived through the disaster, are surrounded by the cause of their trauma. "It's geography," says one psychologist. "With so much coastline, so many islands, there is always, always, a reminder in sight. It's not surprising at all that many people continue to be frightened. Remember, the wave came suddenly—it wasn't a storm. Out of a blue sky, a nice day, there was a tsunami. It's not surprising that people ask themselves, 'If it happened that day, will it happen another day? Tomorrow? Next week?'"[98]

But a lot of Asian fishermen said that the chances of finding other types of work, especially in bad economic times because of the disaster, were remote. They said that although they are not looking forward to fishing again, they do not have a choice. "I'm afraid," says one Thai fisherman, "but I have to do it because my daughter needs an education. I have to fish to send her to school."[99]

Trees, Turtles, and Coral Reefs

In addition to the economic concerns, however, the tsunami caused alarming damage to the environment of Southern Asia, and no one is quite certain what lasting impact that will have. Mangrove trees, for instance, grow in abundance along the coasts, providing secure nesting areas for birds and spawning areas for shellfish. In Indonesia alone, however, more than 60,000 acres of mangroves were destroyed. More than 100,000 acres of farmland, too, were destroyed, and the groundwater underneath was contaminated by tons of saltwater. It will take between five and seven years for the fields and rice paddies to renew themselves. In the meantime, thousands of plantain, coconut, and papaya trees are dying.

Though many species of animals survived the tsunami, sea turtles—which are already on the endangered list—did not fare very well. The youngest turtles lay dead by the hundreds along the coasts, and researchers say that approximately twenty thousand eggs buried in the sand were washed away. With the turtles' nesting areas damaged or destroyed, it was uncertain whether they would survive.

Damage occurred under the water, too. Throughout the region, coral reefs fell victim to the tsunami, as the powerful waves split them and buried many under sand and silt deposits. Coral reefs are valued in the warm tropical waters of Southern Asia both as a tourist attraction for divers and as a rich habitat for fish.

In Indonesia, more than sixty thousand acres of native mangrove trees were destroyed by the tsunami.

Once they have pieced their lives together, tsunami survivors will still live in perpetual fear that another tsunami could strike at any moment.

"We Can Change Disaster into Opportunity"

Interestingly, reefs and other coastal areas are the one aspect of the damaged environment that many experts feel can become a positive thing. The extensive damage of the reefs was made more severe because they had been abused even before the tsunami. Careless divers and rapid overdevelopment of beaches damaged the reefs and the aquatic life within them. There was also too much fishing near the coasts, and as a result, there was damage from boats and nets.

Immediately after the tsunami, the coastal waters, including the reefs, were clogged with trash—everything from cars and refrigerators to pieces of fishing boats. In time, some of the areas may begin to renew themselves. Robert Pomeroy, a marine biology professor at the University of Connecticut, says that the tsunami can be seen as a wake-up call for inhabitants of the region to care for their coastal areas more wisely: "We can change disaster into opportunity now. The fishing and coastal development before the tsunami was unsustainable. We can now start from zero in many communities to work with them to help develop sustainable fishing practices and coastal development that will make their lives better."[100]

The tsunami of December 2004 resulted in an enormous death toll, ongoing trauma and homelessness of millions of Asians, damage to the environment that will surely take years to repair, and the staggering blow to the region's economy. If any good at all is to come from this disaster on a human scale, it will surely be measured by the compassion and generosity that the world demonstrates to the survivors.

Notes

Introduction: "My Heart Doesn't Have Enough Room"

1. Steve Miles, "Banda Aceh: 'Destroyed' Isn't the Word for What Quake, Tsunami Did," *Minneapolis StarTribune*, January 28, 2005.

2. Mark Magnier, "An Undignified Postscript for Sri Lanka's Dead," *Los Angeles Times*, January 14, 2005.

Chapter 1: "The Earth Shrugged for a Moment"

3. Quoted in Evan Thomas and George Wehrfritz, "Tide of Grief," *Newsweek*, January 10, 2005, p. 32.

4. Telephone interview, Paul Meyer, January 22, 2005.

5. Quoted in Michael Elliott, "Sea of Sorrow," *Time*, January 10, 2005, pp. 30–31.

6. Paul Meyer, January 22, 2005.

7. Quoted in John Schwartz, "Sounding the Alarm on a Tsunami Is Complex and Expensive," *New York Times*, December 29, 2004.

8. Quoted in Thomas and Wehrfritz, "Tide of Grief," p. 33.

9. Quoted in Michele Kayal and Matthew Wald, "At Warning Center, Alert for the Quake, None for a Tsunami," *New York Times*, December 28, 2004.

10. Quoted in Elliott, "Sea of Sorrow," p. 35.

11. Quoted in Katy Human, "Warning Systems' Failures Frustrate Colorado Scientists," *Denver Post*, December 31, 2004.

Chapter 2: "I Shall Never Forget the Screaming"

12. Quoted in Andrew C. Revkin, "How Scientists and Victims Watched Helplessly," *New York Times*, December 31, 2004.

13. Quoted in Elliott, "Sea of Sorrow," p. 36.

14. Quoted in Elliott, "Sea of Sorrow," p. 36.

15. Quoted in Simon Elegant, "A City of Debris and Corpses," *Time*, January 10, 2005, p. 38.

16. Quoted in Elegant, "A City of Debris and Corpses," p. 39.

17. Quoted in Elegant, "A City of Debris and Corpses," p. 38.

18. Quoted in Corey Kilgannon, "Tales of Tsunami Survival," *New York Times*, January 2, 2005.

19. Quoted in Joe Eskenazi, "Holiday Turned Nightmare for Berkeley Grad," *Jewish News Weekly*, January 7, 2005, p. 4.

20. Quoted in Eskenazi, "Holiday Turned Nightmare," p. 4.

21. Quoted in Peter Edidin, "A Catastrophe Strikes, and the Cyberworld Responds," *New York Times*, January 2, 2005.

22. Elliott, "Sea of Sorrow," p. 36.

23. Quoted in Thomas and Wehrfritz, "Tide of Grief," p. 32.

24. Quoted in CNN coverage of the tsunami, December 28, 2004.

25. Quoted in Neelesh Misra, "Surviving the Tsunami With Stone Age Instincts," *Minneapolis StarTribune*, January 5, 2005.

26. Quoted in Michael Hanlon, "Did a Sixth Sense Warn Animals of the Great Quake?" *London Daily Mail*, December 31, 2004.

27. Quoted in CNN coverage of the tsunami, December 29, 2004.

28. Quoted in Shawn Donnan, "Bodies Litter the Streets in Town Nearest the Epicenter," *London Financial Times*, December 31, 2004.

29. Quoted in Donnan, "Bodies Litter the Streets," p. 6.

30. Quoted in CNN coverage of the tsunami, December 28, 2004.

31. Quoted in CNN coverage of the tsunami, December 29, 2004.

Chapter 3: Dealing with the Dead

32. Valentine Low, "Where Finding a Friend Is More Likely to Mean Horror Than Hope," *London Evening Standard*, December 31, 2004.

33. Quoted in Nancy Shute, "Now the Second Wave," *U.S. News & World Report*, January 10, 2005, p. 20.

34. Quoted in Elegant, "A City of Debris and Corpses," p. 37.

35. Quoted in James Brooke, "Thais Use Heavy Equipment: Elephants Help Recover Bodies," *New York Times*, January 7, 2005.

36. Brooke, "Thais Use Heavy Equipment."

37. Quoted in Ian Fisher, "Once a Village, Now Nothing," *New York Times*, January 14, 2005.

38. Quoted in Ian Fisher, "In Stench, Amid Ghosts, Seeking the Tsunami Dead," *New York Times*, January 21, 2005.

39. Quoted in Fisher, "In Stench, Amid Ghosts."

40. Quoted in Fisher, "In Stench, Amid Ghosts."

41. Quoted in Bay Fang, "The Aftermath," *U.S. News & World Report*, January 10, 2005, p. 14.

42. Quoted in Kilgannon, "Tales of Tsunami Survival."

43. Quoted in Andrew Marshall, "How to ID the Bodies," *Time*, January 17, 2005, p. 32.

44. Quoted in Marshall, "How to ID the Bodies," p. 33.

45. Quoted in John Burdett, "Thais Have Their Own Response to Tragedy," *Minneapolis StarTribune*, January 18, 2005.

46. Quoted in Fisher, "In Stench, Amid Ghosts."

47. Burdett, "Thais Have Their Own Response to Tragedy."

48. Quoted in Rungrawee Pinyorat, "Tsunami Survivors Live in Fear of Ghosts," *San Jose Mercury News*, January 17, 2005.

Chapter 4: Grief, Guilt, and Pain

49. Quoted in Shute, "Now the Second Wave," p. 20.

50. Quoted in Bill Powell, "After the Flood," *Time*, January 10, 2005, p. 43.

51. Quoted in *Kansas City Infozine*, "For Tsunami Homeless, Sanitation a Critical Concern," January 26, 2005. www.infozine.com/news/stories/op/storiesView/aid/5511.

52. Quoted in Denise Grady, "Even Good Health System Is Overwhelmed by Tsunami," *New York Times*, January 9, 2005.

53. Quoted in Jane Perlez, "For Many Tsunami Survivors, Battered Bodies, Grim Choices," *New York Times*, January 6, 2005.

54. Quoted in Perlez, "For Many Tsunami Survivors."

55. Quoted in Nancy Gibbs, "Race Against Time," *Time*, January 17, 2005, p. 31.

56. Quoted in *The Economist*, "Aceh's Grief," January 8, 2005, p. 26.

57. Quoted in Amy Waldman, "Motherless and Childless," *New York Times*, December 31, 2004.

58. David Rohde, "Tsunami's Cruelest Toll," *New York Times,* January 7, 2005.

59. Quoted in Rohde, "Tsunami's Cruelest Toll."

60. Quoted in Waldman, "Motherless and Childless."

61. Quoted in Unmesh Kher, "Orphaned by the Ocean," *Time*, January 17, 2005, p. 31.

62. Quoted in Jane Perlez and Evelyn Rusli, "Uncounted Costs: Legions of Orphans and Broken Hearts," *New York Times*, January 7, 2005.

63. Quoted in Perlez and Rusli, "Uncounted Costs."

64. Quoted in Deborah Hastings, "Tsunami Orphans in India Face Bleak Futures," *Chicago Sun-Times*, January 26, 2005.

65. Quoted in Hastings, "Tsunami Orphans in India."

66. Quoted in Perlez and Rusli, "Uncounted Costs."

67. Quoted in CBSnews.com, "Tsunami Children Lost, Vulnerable," January 4, 2005. www.cbsnews.com/stories /2005/ 01/04/world/main664712.stml

68. Quoted in Perlez and Rusli, "Uncounted Costs."

69. Quoted in Kher, "Orphaned by the Ocean," p. 31.

Chapter 5: The World Responds

70. Quoted in Elliott, "Sea of Sorrow," p. 34.

71. Quoted in Scott Shane and Nicholas Confessore, "To Those Seeking Help and Giving It, Computer Is a Lifeline," *New York Times*, January 5, 2005.

72. Personal interview, Pam, January 29, 2005, Minneapolis, MN.

73. Quoted in *Chicago Tribune*, "Technology Brings Tragedy Into Americans' Homes," December 31, 2004.

74. Pam, January 29, 2005.

75. Quoted in Elliott, "Sea of Sorrow," pp. 31–32.

76. CNN News, February 2, 2005.

77. Quoted in Bill Powell, "Where Should Your Money Go?" *Time*, January 10, 2005, p. 45.

78. Personal interview, Dion, January 29, 2005, Bloomington, MN.

79. Quoted in Scott Shane, "Pledges Grow, Hurdles Loom in Relief Effort," *New York Times*, January 5, 2005.

80. Quoted in Gibbs, "Race Against Time," p. 32.

81. CNN News, January 4, 2005.

82. Quoted in Gibbs, "Race Against Time," p. 32.

83. Quoted in Melinda Liu, "Getting Relief to Tiger Territory," *Newsweek*, January 17, 2005, p. 33.

84. Quoted in Lely Djuhari, "UN Restricts Aid Workers' Travel," *Minneapolis StarTribune*, January 18, 2005.

85. Quoted in George Wehrfritz and Joe Cochrane, "Charity and Chaos," *Newsweek*, January 17, 2005, p. 31.

86. "Asia's Next Crisis," *Newsday*, January 14, 2005.

Chapter 6: An Uncertain Future

87. Quoted in Powell, "After the Flood," p. 45.

88. Telephone interview, Cassie, February 22, 2005.

89. Quoted in James Brooke, "US Vows to Attain Global Warning System," *New York Times*, January 21, 2005.

90. Quoted in Brooke, "US Vows to Attain Global Warning System."

91. Quoted in Andrew C. Revkin, "Bush Pledges Early Warning System for Atlantic," *New York Times*, January 14, 2005.

92. Quoted in Schwartz, "Sounding the Alarm on a Tsunami."

93. CNN tsunami coverage, January 10, 2005.

94. Quoted in *Economist*, "Back to the Beach," January 8, 2005, p. 55.

95. Quoted in Carrie Chan, "Thai Airline Offers Free Tickets to Lure Tourists," *South China Morning Post*, January 14, 2005.

96. Quoted in Sharon Schmilke, "Boat by Boat, Returning Hope," *Minneapolis StarTribune*, January 23, 2005.

97. Quoted in Elliott, "Sea of Sorrow," p. 39.

98. Telephone interview, Lynn, February 24, 2005.

99. Quoted in Schmilke, "Boat by Boat."

100. Quoted in WTNH.com, "UConn Expert Pressed into Tsuanmi Relief Service," January 23, 2005. www.wtnh.com/Global/category.asp?C=61531.

Organizations to Contact

Pacific Tsunami Warning Center (PTWC)

91-270 Ft. Weaver Rd.
Ewa Beach, Hawaii 96706
www.prh.noaa.gov/ptwc/aboutptw

Established in 1949, the PTWC provides warnings of tsunamis to the Pacific Basin, including Hawaii, Alaska, and the U.S. West Coast. This center, which is part of the National Weather Service, constantly monitors seismic activity in these areas.

Save the Children (STC)

54 Wilton Rd.
Westport, CT 06880
(800) 728-3843
www.savethechildren.org

This nonprofit humanitarian relief organization works in the United States and forty other countries to help children and families improve their health, education, and economic opportunity. STC also mobilizes rapid life-support assistance for children and families caught in tragedies, such as the Southern Asia tsunami.

U.S. Agency for International Development (USAID)

Information Center Ronald Reagan Building
Washington, DC 20523-1000
(202) 712-0000

USAID is the principal U.S. agency to extend assistance to countries recovering from disaster, trying to escape poverty, and engaging in democratic reforms. It is an independent federal government agency that was created in 1961 by President John F. Kennedy.

For Further Reading

Books

Peg Kehret, *Escaping the Giant Wave*. New York: Simon & Schuster, 2000. A fictional account of a tsunami that hits a Pacific resort.

Ellen J. Prager, *Furious Earth: The Science and Nature of Earthquakes, Volcanoes, and Tsunamis*. New York: McGraw-Hill, 2000. Though it has challenging text, the volume contains exceptional maps and illustrations.

Carole Garbuny Vogel, *Shifting Shores*. New York: Franklin Watts, 2003. Good explanation of tectonic plates and their role in the shifting of Earth's surface that can cause an earthquake. Very readable.

Periodicals

Bay Fang, "A Sea Change in Paradise," *U.S. News &World Report*, January 31, 2005.

Brian Murphy, "Search for Missing in Tsunami Presses On," *Seattle Post-Intelligence*, January 26, 2005.

Newsweek International, "Worse Than War," January 17, 2005.

Rebecca O'Connor, "They Needed to Know the World Cared," *Newsweek*, February 14, 2005.

People Weekly, "Wave of Destruction," January 10, 2005.

Rungrawee C. Pinyorat, "Migrant Workers Forgotten Tsunami Victims," *Washington Post*, January 22, 2005.

Internet Sources

Renee Lawrence, "Sri Lanka, Rebels Should Work Together on Tsunami Aid, EU Says," Bloomberg.com, March 9, 2005. www.bloomberg.com/apps/news?pid=10000080&sid=a3Lb8704MI&refer=asia.

U.S. Geological Survey, "Surviving a Tsunami," 1999. www.pubs.usgs.gov/circ/c1187/.

Works Consulted

Periodicals and and Internet Sources

Birmingham Post, "Engineers to Rebuild Tsunami-Hit Villages," January 14, 2005.

James Brooke, "Thais Use Heavy Equipment: Elephants Help Recover Bodies," *New York Times*, January 7, 2005.

———, "US Vows to Attain Global Warning System," *New York Times*, January 21, 2005.

John Burdett, "Thais Have Their Own Response to Tragedy," *Minneapolis StarTribune*, January 18, 2005.

CBSnews.com, "Tsunami Children Lost, Vulnerable," January 4, 2005. www.cbsnews.com/stories/2005/01/04/world/main664712.stml.

Carrie Chan, "Thai Airline Offers Free Tickets to Lure Tourists," *South China Morning Post*, January 14, 2005.

Chicago Tribune "Technology Brings Tragedy Into Americans' Homes," December 31, 2004.

Lely Djuhari, "UN Restricts Aid Workers' Travel," *Minneapolis StarTribune*, January 18, 2005.

Shawn Donnan, "Bodies Litter the Streets in Town Nearest the Epicenter," *London Financial Times*, December 31, 2004.

Economist, "Aceh's Grief," January 8, 2005.

Economist, "Back to the Beach," January 8, 2005.

Peter Edidin, "A Catastrophe Strikes, and the Cyberworld Responds," *New York Times*, January 2, 2005.

Simon Elegant, "A City of Debris and Corpses," *Time*, January 10, 2005.

Michael Elliott, "Sea of Sorrow," *Time*, January 10, 2005.

Joe Eskenazi, "Holiday Turned Nightmare for Berkeley Grad," *Jewish News Weekly*, January 7, 2005.

Bay Fang, "The Aftermath," *U.S. News & World Report*, January 10, 2005.

Ian Fisher, "In Stench, Amid Ghosts, Seeking the Tsunami Dead," *New York Times*, January 21, 2005.

———, "Once a Village, Now Nothing," *New York Times*, January 14, 2005.

Nancy Gibbs, "Race Against Time," *Time*, January 17, 2005.

Denise Grady, "Even Good Health System Is Overwhelmed by Tsunami," *New York Times*, January 9, 2005.

Michael Hanlon, "Did a Sixth Sense Warn Animals of the Great Quake?" *London Daily Mail*, December 31, 2004.

Deborah Hastings, "Tsunami Orphans in India Face Bleak Futures," *Chicago Sun-Times*, January 26, 2005.

Katy Human, "Warning Systems' Failures Frustrate Colorado Scientists," *Denver Post*, December 31, 2004.

Kansas City Infozine, "For Tsunami Homeless, Sanitation a Critical Concern," January 26, 2005. www.infozine.com/news/stories/op/storiesView/aid/5511.

Michele Kayal and Matthew Wald, "At Warning Center, Alert for the Quake, None for a Tsunami," *New York Times*, December 28, 2004.

Unmesh Kher, "Orphaned by the Ocean," *Time*, January 17, 2005.

Corey Kilgannon, "Tales of Tsunami Survival," *New York Times*, January 2, 2005.

Melinda Liu, "Getting Relief to Tiger Territory," *Newsweek*, January 17, 2005.

Valentine Low, "Where Finding a Friend Is More Likely to Mean Horror Than Hope," *London Evening Standard*, December 31, 2004.

Mark Magnier, "An Undignified Postscript for Sri Lanka's Dead," *Los Angeles Times*, January 14, 2005.

Andrew Marshall, "How to ID the Bodies," *Time*, January 17, 2005.

Steve Miles, "Banda Aceh: 'Destroyed' Isn't the Word for What Quake, Tsunami Did," *Minneapolis StarTribune*, January 28, 2005.

Neelesh Misra, "Surviving the Tsunami With Stone Age Instincts," *Minneapolis StarTribune*, January 5, 2005.

Newsday, "Asia's Next Crisis," January 14, 2005.

Jane Perlez, "For Many Tsunami Survivors, Battered Bodies, Grim Choices," *New York Times*, January 6, 2005.

Jane Perlez and Evelyn Rusli, "Uncounted Costs: Legions of Orphans and Broken Hearts," *New York Times*, January 7, 2005.

Rungrawee Pinyorat, "Tsunami Survivors Live in Fear of Ghosts," *San Jose Mercury News*, January 17, 2005.

Bill Powell, "After the Flood," *Time*, January 10, 2005.

———, "Where Should Your Money Go?" *Time*, January 10, 2005.

Andrew C. Revkin, "Bush Pledges Early Warning System for Atlantic," *New York Times*, January 14, 2005.

——— "How Scientists and Victims Watched Helplessly," *New York Times*, December 31, 2004.

David Rohde, "Tsunami's Cruelest Toll," *New York Times*, January 7, 2005.

Sharon Schmilke, "Boat by Boat, Returning Hope," *Minneapolis Star Tribune*, January 23, 2005.

John Schwartz, "Sounding the Alarm on a Tsunami Is Complex and Expensive," *New York Times*, December 29, 2004.

Scott Shane, "Pledges Grow, Hurdles Loom in Relief Effort," *New York Times*, January 5, 2005.

Scott Shane and Nicholas Confessore, "To Those Seeking Help and Giving It, Computer Is a Lifeline," *New York Times*, January 5, 2005.

Nancy Shute, "Now the Second Wave," *U.S. News & World Report*, January 10, 2005.

Evan Thomas and George Wehrfritz, "Tide of Grief," *Newsweek,* January 10, 2005.

Sally Thompson, "Going One-on-One to Help," *Sun Newspapers*, February 24, 2005.

Amy Waldman, "Motherless and Childless," *New York Times*, December 31, 2004.

George Wehrfritz and Joe Cochrane, "Charity and Chaos," *Newsweek*, January 17, 2005.

WTNH.com, "UConn Expert Pressed into Tsunami Relief Service," January 23, 2005. www.wtnh.com/Global/category.asp?C=61531.

Index

Picture Credits

Cover: AFP/Getty Images

© Adress Latif/Reuters/CORBIS, 43, 45
© Anuruddha Lokuhapuarachchi/Reuters/CORBIS, 73
AP Wide World Photos, 8, 15, 24, 37, 40, 50, 68
© Arko Datta/Reuters/CORBIS, 60
© Bazuki Muhammad/Reuters/CORBIS, 47, 63 (inset)
© Beawiharta/Reuters/CORBIS, 58
Corel Corporation, 30, 87
© Costas Synolakis and Jose Borrero, USC, 25, 39, 85
DigitalGlobe Photos, 7 (both), 22 (both)
© Enwaer/XINHUA/CORBIS, 56
© Frederic Larson/San Francisco Chronicle/CORBIS, 55
© Kieran Doherty/Reuters/CORBIS, 52
Maury Aaseng, 11, 13, 80
National Oceanic and Atmospheric Administration, 16, 18
Photos.com, 82, 83
© Pierre Perrin/CORBIS SYGMA, 29
© Reuters/CORBIS, 63 (main)
U.S. Navy photo by Photographer's Mate 1st Class Alan D. Monyelle, 71
U.S. Navy photo by Photographer's Mate 3rd Class Bernardo Fuller, 65
U.S. Navy photo by Photographer's Mate 3rd Class Gabriel R. Piper, 70
U.S. Navy photo by Photographer's Mate Greg Bingaman, 77
U.S. Navy photo by Photographer's Mate 3rd Class Jacob J. Kirk, 19, 33
U.S. Navy photo by Photographer's Mate 3rd Class James McGury, 88
U.S. Navy photo by Photographer's Mate 2nd Class Jeffrey Russell, 51
U.S. Navy photo by Photographer's Mate 1st Class Michael D.
     Kennedy, 66
U.S. Navy photo by Photographer's Mate 2nd Class Philip A. McDaniel,
     74
U.S. Navy photo by Photographer's Mate 3rd Class Rebecca J. Moat, 32
U.S. Navy photo by Photographer's Mate 2nd Class Timothy Smith, 27

About the Author

Gail B. Stewart received her undergraduate degree from Gustavus Adolphus College in St. Peter, Minnesota. She did her graduate work in English, linguistics, and curriculum study at the College of St. Thomas and the University of Minnesota. She taught English and reading for more than ten years. She has written more than ninety books for young people, including a series for Lucent Books called The Other America. She has written many books on historical topics such as World War I and the Warsaw ghetto. Stewart and her husband live in Minneapolis with their three sons, Ted, Elliot, and Flynn; two dogs; and a cat. When she is not writing she enjoys reading, walking, and watching her sons play soccer.